NUMBER 665

THE ENGLISH EXPERIENCE

ITS RECORD IN EARLY PRINTED BOOKS
PUBLISHED IN FACSIMILE

WILLIAM HEALE

AN APOLOGIE FOR WOMEN

OXFORD, 1609

WALTER J. JOHNSON, INC.
THEATRUM ORBIS TERRARUM, LTD.
AMSTERDAM 1974 NORWOOD, N.J.

The publishers acknowledge their gratitude to
the Syndics of Cambridge University Library
for their permission to reproduce the Library's copy
Classmark: Syn.7.60.93, and for permission to
reproduce pages I_3v through I_4f from the Library's
copy, Classmark: Bb*.14.5

S.T.C. No. 13014

Collation: A-I^4

Published in 1974 by

Theatrum Orbis Terrarum, Ltd.
O.Z. Voorburgwal 85, Amsterdam

&

Walter J. Johnson, Inc.
355 Chestnut Street
Norwood, New Jersey
07648

Printed in the Netherlands

ISBN 90 221 0665 9

Library of Congress Catalog Card Number:
74-80185

AN APOLOGIE FOR VVOMEN.

OR

AN OPPOSITION TO Mr. Dr. G. his aſſertion. Who held in the Act at Oxforde. *Anno.* 1608.

That it was lawfull for huſbands to beate their wiues.

By W. H. of Ex. in Ox.

Coloſſ. Chap. 3, verſ. 19.

Huſbands loue your wiues, and be not bitter vnto them.

AT OXFORD,

Printed by Joſeph Barnes Printer to the *Vniverſitie.* 1609.

TO THE HONOVRABLE AND RIGHT-VERTVOVS *Ladie, the Ladie* M. H. all happineſſe.

M*Adam, your commaunde is effected. And this ſhort diſcourſe (the cauſe of whoſe being you are) attẽds your view. In regard whereof, obſequiouſly to begge your kinde acceptance, importes a wronge vnto your courteſie: vtterly to neglect your favourable cenſure, preſumes an overprizing of my labour. To your ſelfe therefore I leaue it: Expectiug from your ſelfe, no other interpretation then as your ſelfe,* faire *and* courteous. *VVhat pleaſeth you not, diſpleaſeth me. The harſh lines you may teach a better language. If anie thing delight, let it ſatiſfie for the manie that may chance to diſlike. If ought offend, let it weare the blacke liverie of your pennes daſh in token of ſorrow. If al through the weakneſſe of argument, debil tate the ſtrenght of ſo good a cauſe, then let all ſuffer for it. For I know that this little body of my apologie is not ſo artificially featured, nor the limbs thereof ſo natural-*

lie iointed, that (as it should) it can seeme a naturall art, or an artificial nature. But your Honors importunity of hast, must beare a part of the blame, together with the shallownes of my cōceipt. And being ioined so sweet a yoake ile easily spurne at Detractiō it self. The truth is, had not your L^s prefixed time dealt sōewhat niggardlie with me, I had dealt more liberallie with it. And those things which now are but sleightlie plaide withall, might haue beene more exactlie handied. Howsoever it is, yours it is: and so shall be ever he from whom it is.

VV H

THE CONTENTS OF THIS APOLOGIE.

ACADEMIA. OXONIENSIS.
SAPIENTIAE: ET.
FELICITATIS.

An Apologie for women.

Chap. I.

An Introduction to the discourse following.

IF in all reason it hath alwaies beene granted, that courtesie may followe after with defence, where discourtesie with offence hath gone before: I cannot thē but imagine this my one only Apologie for women, shall passe your gentle censures, after so many Invectiues framed against them, by their disgracefull adversaries. For although we all know that vnto womankinde the world oweth halfe of its life, and man is indebted the whole of his loue, yet it is a custome growne so common to vnder-valew their worth, as everie rymer hath a libell to impeach their modestie; everie phantastike a poeme to plaine their vnfaithfulnesse; The Courtier though he weare his Mistresse favour, yet stickes not to sing his Mistresse shame; The Cobler though in himselfe most disgracefull, yet wants hee not a ballade for their disgrace. And as this course is vsuall with most men, so the cause hereof is manifest vnto all. The [a] fairest marke (you know) is most often aymed

[a] Seneca. lib.13. ep. 89.

med

med at; & the goodliest starre is most of all gazed vpō: so womā the beautifullst creature of al, is most of al observed. And [b] observatiō as it is sometimes the guide vnto honor, so oftē also it is the mother of disgrace. Particular reasons hereof, many may be collected, out of the many particular humours of such, who stand out in disloialty with them. For some man wil dispraise that woman whom before he adored, because her modestie hath repelled his vnchaste desires. Some will turne their amarous termes of woing into a barbarous stile of rayling, because for want of desert they obtaine not loue. Many loue not women, because they knowe not how to loue them. And most of all men being evil themselues, loue but few things that are good, and so perchance hate women also. Some likewise to make ostentation of their wit vnto the stage. Few vpon anie shew of reason. None (I dare avouch) vpon anie iust cause, haue yet filled the world with pamphlets, things most idle in themselues, and most disgracefull vnto women. But ô vnmanlike men, and staine of your sexe! Is this a point of your manhood, or anie ornament of your valour, to busie your selues for disgrace of womē, whom nature hath disarmed of corporal strenght, and education disabled of mental courage for revenge? Js this the thankful tribute you repaie vnto the author of your being? Js this the sweete imbracement you bestow on the paps that gaue you sucke? Js this the grateful allowance you afforde them for their sorrow and paines at your birth, for

[b] Tacitus hist 3. lib ad princip:

their

their care and diligence in your youth, for their loue and carefulnesse through-out your life? All such [a] courtesies (me seemes) should not be so vngratefullie forgotten, much lesse iniuriouslie remembred. But why talke I with these men of gratitude the greatest of vertues, who never were acquainted with anie vertue at al? And therfore had it beene the highest of womens misfortune, to haue beene traduced by this infamous crew, they might easilie haue smil'd it out; counting no dishonour to be evil-spoken of by them, who never learn'd to speake well of anie. But nowe this bad cause hath gotten better patrones: especially whē in the Vniversitie, in the open Act, in publike disputation their names are called in question, their capacitie thought vnfit for learning, themselues adiudged worthie of blowes. To let passe the rest; what more strange and prodigious paradoxe? What opinion more vnnaturall and vncivill then this of theirs, *That it is lawfull for a husband to beate his wife?*

Most impure hart [b] which did first conceiue, & more then most barbarous tongue, [c] which did afterward bring forth such a monster of opinion. Had I but one word to speake, (saue onlie my orizons;) but one onlie line to write, I woulde both speake and write them in defiance hereof.

[a] Ausonius de grat. action. ad Aug.

[b] Diabolus hic fuit, vt opinatur Chry hom 57. in 29. Gen. vbi ait Diabolus subingressus tantum in eis damnum facit, vt quotidianæ lites aut pugnæ inter eos nascentur.

[c] Cyclopes fuerūt illi, vt conijciunt quidē doctissimi viri, ex Hom. lib 9. Odiss. hoc dicto de Cyclop. --lus quisq; ministrat Prognatis ac vxoribus.

Chapt. 2.

That it is not lawful for a husband to beat his wife, is proved by reasons drawne from Nature.

AND to begin first, whence we al began, from *Nature* her selfe. Her eternal law stampt frõ the worldes beginning in all her creatures, witnesseth such a soveraigne vnion of male and female, that in al kindes betweene thẽ there is found no vnkindnesse.

Translat. ex Strozio laur. poet. vbi incipit. Non solet in dominã leo trix saevire leaenam, &c.

No [a] Lions rage against the Lionesse:
The Tygre to the Tygresse is not fierce:
No Eagles doe their fellow birds oppresse:
The hauke doth not the hauke with talẽts pierce:
All couples liue in loue by natures lore,
VVhy should not man & wife do this, & more?

Man the great creators greatest creature indued with *Remembrance* a register to recount former events: with *wisdome* a glasse to behold the present estate of things; with *Providence* an oracle to coniecture of future accidents: aboue al with *Reason* a ballance to weigh out al his actions: must now become more cruell and tyranous, nay more savage & barbarous, then verie beasts, who neither haue remembrance of things past, wisedome in thinges present, providence of things to come, nor reason in anie thing at al. The [b] *Doues* are observed to be most exquisite in their loue, and at the fatal departure of one, the other pines to death with sorrow. The [c] *Nightingall* makes pleasant melody in his loues wel-fare, but in her distresse he mournes in sadder tunes. The [d] *Swanne* is of a nature sutable to his feather, white and faire, and al his feare is, to keepe his mate from feare. Go therefore into the fields, & the *Doues* wil read thee a lecture of loue:

[b] Plin. nat. hist. li. 10. c. 24.

[c] Plin. nat. li. 10. c. 29.

[d] Strobeus vt recitat Patricius & Plin. nat. hist. lib. 10. ca. 23.

returne

returne into the woodes, and the *Nightingals* wil sing thee madrigals of loue: walke by the riuer, & the *Swannes* wil schoole thee the art of loue: every where such loving couples in brutish beasts will shame the disagreeing matches in reasonable creatures. For shal the bare instinct of a sensible nature worke so powerfully in this case with beasts, as none are found so beastly to infringe it; and shal the helpe of a purer essence take none effect in mã and he not adiudged worse then a beast? The [a] *Lion* that spareth no creature, is said to tremble at a woman, and hardly profferеth her that violence, which vsually he doth to man: as though *Nature* had taught him a more gentle behaviour towards so faire a personage, or his owne heroicke spirit to scorne of so base a victorie.

[a] Plin. li. 8. natur. hist.

[b] *For never gotten was immortal fame,*
By working of a silly womans shame.

[b] Translat. è Virgil. Aenead. 2. Nullũ memorabile nomen foemineâ in poenâ est.

The [c] *Viper* a beast more vile then the vilest, poisonous by nature, and spitefull, odious to be seene and hatefull; Yet when the time of his breeding approacheth, withdrawes himselfe vnto the sea or rivers side, and by the gentle murmurre of his knowne hisse calleth fourth the Lãprey with whõ his nature is to ingender. The Lamprey being so kindly invited, doth as kindly repaire vnto him. Whom when he perceiveth comming to accept of his loue, vomiteth forth al his poison; doing reverence (as it were) vnto his nuptial rightes: and casting away his natural corruption, meeteth his spouse in his cleanest perfection. Man would take

[c] S. Ambrosius. tom. 1. lib. 5. cap. 7 Hexa m. & Arist. de hist. anim.

ſcorne to be thought worſe then a *Viper*, and why then ſcorneth he not to caſt out of his hart, all his cancred poiſon of anger, of ſtrife, of fighting, of quarrelling, when he commeth into his Miſtreſſe preſence? To be plaine a dogge wil not ſo much as bite his mate, & ſhall a husband beat his wife, and be not therein worſe then a dogge? If not, then vnhappy is the people, and infortunate the common wealth; where the liberty ſhal be more large, and more licentious the laws of men then of beaſts.

d Plato in Phædon & M T Cicero in Lelio Natura optima recte vivẽdi dux.

It may wel be the worlds motto,[d] *All thinges haue Nature for their guide*. And of this al, eſpecily Man the worlds commaunder: which we may obſerue, as in the cõmon courſe of life; in ordering his diet, in wearing his apparell, in taking his reſt: ſo likewiſe in the perfit habite of ſciences; in his ſmoothing Rhetoricke, in his ſollide diſputation, in his profound Philoſophy. In al which the greateſt prehemineñce, *Art* can challenge, is to [e] adde perfection where *Nature* hath laid a foundation. The law then being an artificial collection of naturall precepts, how can it diſpenſe with ſo vnnaturall an action; as for a huſband to beate his wife, the other part of himſelfe, nay his other-ſelfe, or his better halfe? No [f] man did ever willingly hurt himſelfe; or if any man hath, certainely he maie iuſtlie of all men bee helde a madde man: and therefore what mutual blowes can lawfully paſſe betweene mã & wife; who are one and the ſelfeſame? Their mindes inſeparably one in their loue & amity: their bodies individually the ſame in their childrẽ & poſteritie.

e Ariſtot. Phy. 2.

f Ariſt. Eth. lib. 5.

Jndeed ſome ancient ages of barbariſme (before either civillity was fully imbraced, or chriſtianitie firmely eſtabliſhed) ſeemed to draw from *nature* the practiſe of ſome ſuch tyrannie. So [a] *Ariſtotle* reportes of the Scythians: [b] *Tacitus* of the Germans: [c] *Gellius* of the Romaines: [d] *Cæſar* of the French: with whom it was a received cuſtome to diſpoſe of their wiues both life and libertie, according to their pleaſure. And hence it was that M[r]. Doctor ſeemed to alleadge his hiſtory of [e] *Publius Sēpronius* who divorced his wife for ſeeing a play. Of [f] *Egnatius* * *Mecennius* who beate his wife for being found in his cellar. Of [g] *Faunus* who killed his wife for drinking a cup of wine. Fit prooſes for confirmation of ſuch a truth. Recount the time, it was in paganiſme and a barbarous age: Obſerue the perſons, they lived as mirrors of rigour & cruelty, & are regiſtred as the monumēts of murther and tyrannie. Weigh the reaſons that moued thē thereunto, they will ſooner caſt you into laughter, then perſwade you of imitation. Laſtly iudge of al and all is but as though a Phyſition ſhould go into an Apothecaries ſhop, where is variety of wholeſome medicines, yet preſcribes hee ſome poyſon ſome drudge to ſtrēgthē his ſicke patient. Right ſo M[r]. Doctor travailed over divers hiſtories where was diverſity of good examples, yet produceth he the worſe of all to ſhoulder vp his weake opnion. Farre better befitting the place, more plauſible to your auditory, and no leſſe gracious for your ſelfe, had beene the famous examples of loving

[a] Ariſt 1. lib Pol. cap 1.
[b] Cornel. Tac. lib de moribus German.
[c] Aul. Gell. lib. 10 c. 2. de Roman. antiquit.
* Metellus vt alij.
[d] Cæſar cōment lib. 6 de bello Gallic.
[e] Stobæus ex quo recitat Patr. lib 4. tit 3. & Bodin. de rep. 1.
[f] Plinius li. 14. cap 13.
[g] Arnobius lib. 5. contra gentes.

husbands towardes their wiues, of louing wiues towardes their husbandes, or of either louing towards the other. How welcome would haue bin the very name of *Hector*? [h] who in the destruction of *Troie*, did indeed bewaile the death of *Priamus*, the sacking of so great a city, the spoile of so many deare and valiant brethren, the funerals of so faire & large an Empire: but exceeded all excesse in lamenting *Andromache* his wife, and desired (saith *Homer*) to forsake heauen being already seated among the Gods, to defend *Andromache* distressed here on earth. How pleasant had been the rehearsal of [i] *Tygranes* loue, who with his beloued Queen being taken prisoner by *Cyrus*, made a free and liberal promise of his life, to purchase her ransome? What good entertainment had the storie of [a] *Calenus* had, who thought he liued no longer, then when he looked on his beloued wife? In how faire a language woulde [b] *Livie* haue spoken for you, of *Augustus*, of *Antonius*, of *Scævola*, of *Aruntius*, of *Scipio*, of *Marius*, and [c] other histories of infinite other, whom for this cause, posteritie hath aduanced aboue men, if not honoured as Gods?

And howbeit in womẽ the sexe be weaker, yet not their loue. Witnesse [d] *Cornelia* who so dearely affected her *Pompey*, that she would not suffer him to go into the warres (though he were the worldes terrour) vnlesse her selfe in presence might waite vpon him. Witnesse [e] *Demotia*, who hauing lost her *Leosthenes* could not finde her selfe, and therefore through solitarinesse made a speedy voyage vn-

[h] Hom. Ill 5
[i] Zenoph. in Cyro ∣∣o.
[a] Martial. in epigram. illo. O molles tibi quindecim Calene, &c.
[b] Tit. Livius in diver locis hist ab vrbe condita.
[c] Frontinus in 4. l strat. de P. Serv. Suet. in Tiberio de C. Attilio. Zonaras de T. Sempronio Polib. in 3 lib. de M. Pomponi, &c.
[d] Lucan vbi se pel icem sul æ vo antem inducit.
[e] D Hieronim. in Iov

vnto death after him. Witnesse [f] *Su'pitia*, who being adiudged to stay, and watched that she should stay at *Rome*, when her husband *Lentulus* was banished frõ *Rome*, yet (notwithstanding the *Senates* commande, her princely fathers charge, the loue of her citie and country, the losse of friends & family) shee alone exposed her selfe vnto the dãger of the night, beguiled the watchfull eies of her stricte guarde, brake forth of the city, and lackied him along the fields, vntil shee became the ioieful companion of his woful banishment. So little she esteemed all the worldes felicity in regarde of one *Lentulus*, and for one *Lentulus* so willingly she incurred whatsoever misery. Witnesse [g] *Panthea*, *Rhodogune*, *Laodemia*, *Martia*, *Valeria*, *Portia*, *Lucretia*, [h] *Penelope*, [i] *Alcinoe*. Millions of like, whose singular fame herein, as it hath caused antiquity to invest them in the eternal shrines of honour: so might likewise their reheatsall enforced posteritie to receiue thẽ as the fruitful patternes of imitatiõ.

[f] E Plin. lib 10 c. 3. recitat D. Hieron. ibid.

[g] De quibus D. Hierom. to. 2 lib. 1. contra Iouianum.

[h] Ovid. in ep. Pen. ad vlis.

[i] Ovid Metamorph. li. 11. fa. 10.

But to returne to your alleadged histories: who imagines it not a simple house, that is built on such rotten posts? And who sees it not a weake defence (God wot) that hath so vnworthy props? Graunt your writers relation to be true: yet how thence proue you the action to bee lawful? Since al was done vnadvisedly without discussing of the matter, wrongfully without the hearing of a iudge, wilfully without any giving of sentence, [k] al which the law requires. These then being savage & heathenish murders both against *Nature*, and the law

[k] Iustin. instit lib. 4. tit. de iud.

of

of *Nations*, let me demaunde who received the greater foile, either the tyranous husbands which rashly abused, or the modest wiues which patiently endured? If you saie the latter, where is your iudgement? If the former, of what force then is your argument? But not to trace you too farre in your owne field: Giue me leaue to remoue your case into the court of Morallity, or civil Pollicie; where if the Jurie passe with you, you shall haue cause stil to imbrace it: if not, you haue no reason longer to fancie it.

Chap. 3.

The same confirmed by the rules of Morallity or Civill Pollicie.

Marriage of al humane actions is the one & only weightiest. It is the present disposall of the whole life of man: it is a [a] *Gordian* knot that may not bee loosed but by the sworde of death: it is the ring of vnion whose poesie is *Pure* and *endlesse*. In a word it is that state which either imparadizeth a man in the Eden of felicitie, or els exposeth him vnto a world of miserie.[b] Hence it is that so mature deliberatiō is required, before such an eternal bond be vnited. The mutual affection of each partie, the consent of parents, the approbation of friends, the trial of acquaintance: besides the especial obseruance of disposition, of kindred, of education, of behaviour. Now then if a man so-

[a] Boindus de rep. li. 1.

[b] Dr. Casus observat. ex veteribus in com. in Oecon Arist. lib 2.

lem.

lemnize marriage vpon these due respects, he can hardly make his choice amisse, because hee is guided by vertue which never faileth her followers. But if not, he maie well bee styled a foole, because he is carried awaie with passion, which easilie impoisoneth the best designes. The man therefore that is truely wise cannot but choose a vertuous wife, and so by consequent liue quietly with her. And if any take a vicious woman, it argues his owne folly, and so by good reason may patientlie endure her. For now he hath, but that which before he desired, and he desired that which then he fancied; though indeede not from the informance of a true iudgement, but by the inducement of a giddy affection.

And yet in this infortunate case, it is the greatest folly of al follies, for a man to aggrandize his owne misfortunes by quarreling with his owne choise. For that dissention taketh away the very end and vse of marriage, debarreth from all comfort and vtility thereof, banisheth its ioy and felicity, no man is so ignorant but he may wel knowe, none so obstinat but he must needs acknowledge. What wife is there so absolutely void of all passionate spleen, who wil so lovingly performe her mariage-rites, so carefully bring vp her children, so providently order her house, so diligently direct her servants, for a disagreeing as for a loving husband?[a] VVho wil buy blowes as deare as shee will pay for loue? Or what husband is there so cleare without gal, that wil so intentiuely augment his

a Plautus in Picudolo.

patrimonie, so warily imploie his stocke, so heedy-lie follow his affaires, so wel in al things vse al his diligence, for a wife whom he loatheth, as for her whom he loveth? [b] Who wil be as devout a beadsman to the Saint he fansieth not, as to him whom he chiefly adoreth? So that indeed neither (as they shoulde) caring for the other, both receiue an infinite dãmage to themselues; and for their posterity leaue it most infortunat. Infortunat in their birth, for feare their dissentious parents derived to them their dissentious, spirites. Infortunate in their education, for feare their backward parents hindered their instruction. Infortunate in their estate for feare their carelesse parents diminished their portions. Infortunat in their credit, infortunate in al, for feare least al their parents faults redound vnto the childrẽs paine. Whẽ as in agreeing matches, where man and wife make vp the sweet harmonie of mutual loue, in a reciprocal consent and vnion; yee may obserue a heauen of gouernmẽt, the husband intent on his businesse, the wife imploied in her house, their children brought vp religiously, their attendãts, their servants, euery one (as [c] *Virgils* common-wealth of Bees) busied in his place. Whence towardes the autumne of their yeeres, they gather in the fruitfull haruest of true friendshippe, of competent riches, of good estimation, of selfe-content.

[b] Tacit. annalium l. 2.

[c] Virg. Aenead lib. 1.

But let vs discarde those vtilities a while. And suppose thy wife not as thy wife, but as a woman only. Tel me then I praie (since [d] euerie action of

[d] Arist. li. 3. Eth. cap. 1.

man

man must bee tutored by some vertue or other) what appearaunce of vertue can it be for a man to beate a woman? It is not [e] *valour*, because that demands equallitie of cōbatants. It is not [f] *wisdome*, because that depends on a staide carriage. It is not [g] *Iustice*, because that requires a serious deliberation: not [h] *Temperance*, because that wants vnsetled passion. And if none of these, then no vertue at all: [i] for all other vertues are comprised vnder them, as some lesser dignitie vnder a more ample stile. Tel me likewise to what end should men attempt such violence? If a woman be perverse, shee thereby amendeth not; if gentle, shee deserues it not: if you seeke praise thereby, you shal merit laughter: if rewarde, you shal be sure of shame. Whereas therefore you are guided by no vertue, nor directed vnto anie end, who but stonie hearts will laie their violent hands on a womā the patterne of innocencie, the Queene of loue, the picture of beauty, the Mistresse of delight? who could with blows deface those rich ornamēts of nature? Who could quarrel with her cheekes so purely mixt with Lillies and Roses? Who could violate those eies the spheares of light and loadstars of affection? Who could wrong those lips such rubies of value, and rivers of delight? Who would not imagine those ivorie armes fitter for imbracing then buffeting? And who but thinke those snowy hands more apt for a seamsters needle, then a fencers chudggle.

> [k] *Beauty must not acquaint her with the warres;*
> *And therefore hates such men, as loue such iars.*

[e] Cicero in offficijs lib. 1. c. de fortitud.

[f] Idem lib. 2 offic. ad princip.

[g] Idem li. 1. offic. circ. medium.

[h] Idem l. 2. officiorum.

[i] Idem offic lib. 1. tract. de fortit.

[k] Translat. è Petron. vbi incipit Non . mat. arma venus, &c.

And howbeit al women are not beautiful, neither hath nature bestowed al perfections on every wife: yet a true-louing husband must imagine thē al in his truly beloued wife.[1] For loue esteemes not a thing beloved, as in it selfe it is; but as it appeares in the lovers eie. And therfore a womā that is not faire, may yet make a faire wife, in regard of her husbande; as if shee be only faire in her husbandes thought. For he sees her with his owne (not with others) eies: loues her only with his owne hart; inioies her only to his own content; in her then whō need he to please but himselfe? So that if thy wife bee not fairer to thy-selfe then other women are, thou lovest her not truelie. And if thou lovest her not, why diddest thou accept a loathed companion? Why diddest thou dissemble with God before whom thou professedst loue? Why diddest thou lie vnto Man, in whose presence thou promisedst loue? Or if shee be, (as indeed shee should be) fairer in thine owne eie, because dearer to thine own heart, with what art canst thou turne rebel vnto loue, & whom before thou lovedst, presently hate her: or remaining constant with what face canst thou looke vpon thy beloued, and instantlie beate her? No, no: heauen may assoone sinke into hel as perfect loue turne into hatred: and whole rivers of water may aswel spring out of flames of fires, as violent blowes proceede frō fervent loue. In a word therefore, if thou louest not thy wife, thou haste plaide the hypocrite, and so with shame maist beate her. But if thou louest her, thou haste

[1] S. Phillip. Syd. Arcad lib. 2.

per-

performed thy vow, and so with due respect must honour her.

Neither may it be thought a smal reason to deter al husbands from such violence, to forecast the dangers that may ensue thereof. For diverse women being of a diverse stature, strength, complexion and disposition, there must needes fal out a diverse event of such an action. As for other men I dare not speake: and for Mr. Dr. I know not what may befall: but if I shoulde chaunce to marrie with a stoute and valiant woman, such as either [m] *Penthesilaa* was amongst the *Amazons*, or the Lady [n] *Parthenia* of *Greece*, or the Empresse [o] *Livia* in *Rome*, or some other of farre lesse valour: & after a while from *Cupids* warres fal vnto Martial armes, J doubt my learning woulde not saue mee from some vnlearned blowes. Jf I shoulde accept of a weake and feeble wife, such an one whose courage is daunted with a worde, whose Jnnocence is her defence, whose yeelding her resistance, and yet play the Tyrant stil, and so dispatch her; I am sure my law wil not free mee from the tribunall of heaven, howsoever it cleare mee from the iudgement of man. Suppose I shoulde marrie a modest matrone, whose speech, gate, carriage, and behaviour are as cleare as Christall, all without blemish, and yet al please mee not without some ciuil warres, howe shoulde I liue offensiue to my friendes, vpbraided by mine enemies, of most men hated, beloued of none. Lastly if I should light on a light hus-wife, who yet being civilly en-

[m] Virg. Aenead lib. 1.
[n] Sr Phil. Syd. Arch. lib 3.
[o] Aerodius rerum iudicatarum lib. 8. cap. 8.

treated, might civilly demaine her selfe, but being trodden vpon (as everie worme) wil turne againe: how iustly might I weare [p] *Vulcans* night-cappe on [q] *fooles holydaies*, and in sad devotion do perpetual homage vnto the [r] new moone. Now therefore a farre safer course it is for vs, to lay aside our weapons, and rest in tearmes of loue, then to vẽture our selues in so doubtful a ieopardy. And let our wiues bee what they be, it is our wisdome now to loue them, since it was our fortune first to haue them.

[p] Vide Heroditum in Melpomone.
[q] Vide T. Livium lib. 45. hist. ab vrbe cond. ad finem.
[r] Vide Ovid. Amorũ

And as the private event of this action must needs be inconvenient vnto our selues, so the publike example thereof is dangerous vnto the common-wealth. For whatsoever in this kinde is committed within our own family, is acted (as it were) on an open theater, where wee haue store of spectators: our children, our servants, our neighbors, sometimes our nearest kindred, oft times our dearest friends. Who perchance (as most men are) being ready to followe the ill [s] example of others, may proue by little and little the verie abstracts of impietie. Especially when in this case we haue experience of so many cruel & execrable murders. Some through open tyranie, as of [t] *Pompeia* by *Nero*; some through secret villanie, as of [u] *Apronia* by *Sylvanus*: some through strangling: some through poisoning: some through falle accusing: too too manie through pining awaie at their husbands vnkindnes. With al which kindes I could haue wished that this our white *Albion* had never

[s] Vt habet Iuven. Sat. 13. Velocius & citius nos corrũpunt vitiorum exempla domestica, magnis cũ subeant animos authoribus.
[t] Plutarch. in lib. Connub.
[u] Vives ita recitat in l. de off. mar

been

beene bespotted. Now in those hainous crimes though thy selfe perchance abhorrest to bee an actor, yet to teach the principles which breed these conclusions, or to be the exemplarie cause which bringeth forth these effects, wil appale anie morall man, and touch a christians conscience. For faultie is he that giues the occasiō, as wel as he who commits the action; seeing men are as greedy to catch at opportunity, as a fish to leape at the hooke, especiallie when the one hath a pretence of law, as the other a shew of baite.

Besides it is a maine hinderance to anie publike preferment, for how can he be thought fit to manage the affaires of a common wealth, who is not able to keepe orders in his owne house? How can he wel preserue peace among the vnconstant many, who is at daily strife in his owne family? [u] *Gordias* the Rhetoritian made an oratiō vnto the *Grecians* being then in some ciuil broiles, to perswade them vnto concord; and having generally wonne the harts of both sides, *Melantius* his adversarie replied. O yee foolish *Grecians*, is this fellow fit to perswade you concorde, who liues himselfe in perpetual dissention? Can he rule the whole cittie (thinke you) in peace, where are so many diverse mindes, as there are divers men; and was yet neuer able to gouerne his house in quiet, where are none but his wife and himselfe? Which speech of his to this effect, so possessed the people, that what before they were fully perswaded of, they now but faintly believed, & so by degrees falling into a per-

[u] S Hieronimus li 1. contra Iuli. anū tom. 2.

fit

fit relapse of discorde; whereas at the beginning they entertained him with good applause, in the end they hissed him frõ the barre with this acclamation. *Gordias rule thy selfe first at home, then after rule vs at Olympia.* Neither was this *Gordias* his fortune only, but it is a common brand of infamie to al his followers; who alwaies by their il priuate carriage draw vnto thẽ suspition of their like publike government.

[a] Herodotus in Clio.

Wherefore antiquity hath beene verie provident herein. [a] When as the chiefe guests at their marriage-feasts, vsed to offer sacrifice for those that were married. But before they came vnto the altar, they purified their oblation from its gal, and spiced it with fragrant odours. A custome in my sense not so ceremonious, as iudicious, whose moral is given by the [b] best moralist to pretend a duety of man and wife, that in them should bee no gal or bitternes, but the sweete relish of pleasing loue. They themselues should bee as [c] *Virgils* vine and elme, the tendernes of the one supported by the others strenght. Their hearts as [d] *Leda's* twins both interchangeably imbracing each other. Their house as [e] *Plato's* citty, wherein nothing must bee called *mine* or *thine*; but all things common vnto them both: nothing peculiar to the husband, nothing propper to the wife, which vpon eithers occasion is not to be imparted to the other. And if those singular pares and paralels of friends (whose fame with golden wings flies throughout the world,) nothing was singular, al things mutual: in

[b] Plutar. in Cõnubial.
[c] Virgilij Egloga 5. vitis vt arboribus decus est, &c.
[d] Ovidius lib. 6 Met.
[e] Plat. in 1. lib. de repub. siue de iusto.

prosperity mutual ioy;mutual sorrow in adversity: in adventures mutual aide;mutual triumph in victories:in al things mutual loue the mother of al this mutuallity? What lesse can we expect in mariage, a stronger bond then friendship,where to the present fruition of a friendly mate,is added the hopeful expectatiō of future issue? Now we never read nor heard of any of those friends who gaue a blow vnto his friend,either moved therevnto on violēt passiō,or otherwise induced by any occasiō. Why then should husbands sue for a toleration to beate their wiues, to whom as they are in society more nearely linked , so in loue more dearely engaged then to their dearest friend?Many are the friendly offices of thy friend;many more of thy wife. Shee sits at thy table:shee lies in thy bosome: she shares of thy grievances and lessens the burden:shee participates thy pleasures and augments the ioy: in matters of doubt shee is thy counseller;in case of distresse thy comforter : shee is a cō-partner with thee in al the accidents of life. * *Neither is there any* sweeter taste of friendship, then the coupling of soules in this mutuallity either of condoling or comforting : where the oppressed minde findes it selfe not altogither miserable,since it is sure of one which is feelingly sorry for his misery. And the ioiful spends not his ioy either alone, or there where it may be envied : but freely sends it to such a wel grounded obiect, from whence he shal be sure to receiue a sweet reflexion of the same ioie. And as in a cleare mirrour of sincere goodwil see a liuely

* S.Phill. Sydn.Arcad lib. 3.

picture of his owne gladnes. For which cause especially (as I conceiue) *Isocrates* [a] cōdemnes him for most lewdly disposed, who by his faire speech and close demainour hath wooed a virgin, & in pomp & Ioviality married her his wife, will yet through anger or folly liue at variance with her. [b] *Seneca* termes the brawls in marriage worse then divorce from marriage. [c] *Cato* plainely cals it sacriledge for a husband to beat his wife. Such as is the soule (saith [d] *Plutarch*) in regard of the body, such is the husband in respect of his wife, both do liue in vniō, in disiunction both doe perish. [e] True loue is the best amatorie or chiefest medicine to breede true loue: [f] And therefore if thou looke truely to be beloved of thy wife, first loue her truely: for els howe canst thou require that for thy selfe of her, which thou affordest not frō thy selfe vnto her. She may in this case answere thee as [g] *L. Crassus* the Senator replied on *L. Philippus* the Cōsul; how should I shew my selfe a Senator vnto you, whereas you behaue your selfe not as a Consull towardes mee? How should a wife proue loving vnto her husband when as her husband proues not loving vnto her? For both in loue and friendship the demaunde of *Martial* vnto his *Marcus* stāds with good reason.

[h] *If Pylades thou wilt me haue,*
Then (Marke) *Ile thee Orestes craue.*
And not in words thou must it proue;
VVilt be belov'd then thou must loue.

Loue is a relation, and must haue two subiects for its residence, as wel the husband as the wife: if it finde

[a] Isocrates in Symmi.
[b] Sen. li. ad Gallionem de remedijs fort.
[c] Plu. in vita Censorij Cat.
[d] Plut. li. de præceptis connubial.
[e] Lodo. Vives in li de offic mar.
[f] Sen. ep. 9 ad Luciliū.
[g] Valerius lib. 6. cap. 2
[h] Martia. epig. lib 6. Translatio cius vt præstem Pyladen aliquis mihi præstet orestes Hoc non fit verbis, Marce vt ameris ama.

finde not good intertainment with one, it departs from both. Both therefore must be like *Crateres* and *Hyparchia*,[i] who were said to see with double eies, because in mutual loue they acquainted one the other with passage of al things that concerned them. So that as the Prophets in *Israell* were sacredly intitled [k] *Seers*, because they had a double sight, of nature and from God: so was *Crateres* in Athens iestingly tearmed a [l] *Seer*, because he vsed a double sight, his wiues and his owne.

[i] Vide Lodovicum Vivem de off mar.

[k] ..Sam.9.6

[l] Ἐπιπηκτής. [illegible]

And howsoever we exclaime against women, that they are vnworthy of such respect by reason of the multiplicitie of their supposed infirmities: Such words often flash forth indeed, but from the pregnancie of wit, not from the soundnes of iudgment: spoken either from a preiudicate opinion, which ever miscarieth, or from particular example, which neuer concludeth. For instance we may hold them vnconstant in their resolutions, shallow in their iudgment, lavish of their tongue, and with so many weaknesses beweaken this weake sexe, as that we may reviue that old theorem hissed long agoe from of the stage of vertue,

> [m] *Of women-kinde found good ther's none:*
> *And if perchance there be found one;*
> *I know not how it comes to passe,*
> *The things made good that evill was.*

[m] Transl. veteris car. Fœmina nulla bona est, vel si bona contigit vni, Nescioquo pacto res mala facta bona est.

A flat impiety against the al Creators al sufficiencie. Who when hee had built this worlds faire house, lookt in every corner thereof, & saw that al was good, yet they in the fairest roome of all, haue found that al is naught. And if you flie from their first vnspotted creation vnto their now corrupted dispositiõ, what priviledge haue men beyond women? They are both made of one mettal: cast both in the same mould: al are not good, nor the most best. But if any might challendge preheminence it should seeme the woman might, whose complexion is purer, which argues a richer wit; whose passions are weaker, which pretend a more vertuous disposition. In fine therfore dislike of them we cãnot, whom nature hath every way so curiously framed, vnlesse we more dislike of our selues, who are the monuments of her rougher workmanship.

Yet for your pleasures sake, suppose women to be as bad as you would haue thẽ. Say they are past al vertuous modesty: sweare they are beyonde al hopeful recovery. Be it so. I demand thẽ, wherfore should they be beatẽ? [n] None but final punishmẽt is there to be inflicted, where the person punished cannot be amended. Women (say you) are past amendment, and therefore (say I) they are past punishment. It [o] is an axiome in Philosophy, that where the cause is takẽ awaie, the effect perisheth, [p] and it is againe as firme a position in humanitie, that amendment is the chiefe (if not sole) cause of everie such punishment: There being thẽ no hope of the one, there ought likewise be no exaction of the other. Now that womẽ wil never be amended it is as commõ a phrase in our adversaries mouth, as *what lacke yee* in the *Exchange*. So that it was growne long since vnto a proverbe.

[n] S. Aug. li. 19. de civitate Dei.

[o] Arist. in 1. lib. physic.

[p] Sen lib. 1. de clemẽtia. Et Gell. noct. Attic. lib. 6. c. 14.

[q] *They wash a ieat*
To make it white as snow:
VVho women beat
To make them vice forgoe. Lastly [r] *Aristotle* (whose words are maximes in Philosophy, & his *Ipse dixit* an authentical proofe) seemeth herein to soare aboue himselfe, & leaving his wōted schoole of humanity, to speake frō out the sacred chaire of divinity. *The divine prouidēce*, (saith he) so framed mā & womā, that they of necessity must be of one society, otherwise how could they perpetuate the worlde by their offsprings succession, since neither man without woman, nor woman without man cā haue any issue? Wherefore they were made both like, & yet dislike: like in specifical nature, their bodies of the like feature, their soules of the same essence. Dislike in the Individual, the one hotter and drier, th'other colder & moister, that out of this disagreeing cōcord of a divers tēper, should proceed the sweet harmony of agreeing loue. The one strōger, the other weaker, that the stronger in loue should demaine himselfe more roially; the weaker for feare should behaue her-selfe more curteously. The one valiant & laborious in the fields; the other milde & diligēt within the dores: that what the one had painfully gottē abroad, the other might carefully cōserue at home. The one fairer, & as a delightsome picture of beauty: the other more sterne, & as a perfit mirror of manhood. The one more deepely wise, the other of a more pregnant wit. Both which being by the sacred power of mariage made

[q] Transl. prove. car. Ille lavat laterem qui castigat mulierem.
[r] Arist. in Oecon. lib. 1. c 3. & 4.

[a] Idem.ibid
c 4 vbi le-
ges mariti
erga vxo-
res consti-
tuit.
[b] Vt memi-
nit. Plat. in
Gorgia &
Arist hoc
in loco.

but one, the [a] first condition of their *Vniō* is, *That no wrong should be done by either to the other.* For by the [b] *Pythagorians* law of hospitalitie it was decreed, that *None who entered into an others house, should for the time of his aboad there, suffer any kind of iniury vpon any occasion.* A husband taketh his wife from her friends, disacquainteth her with her kindsfolkes, debarreth her her parents sight, and estrangeth her from whomsoever was dearest vnto her; he takes her into his own hospitality; receiues her into his own protection, & himselfe becomes her sole Guardian. Wherefore then to beate and abuse her, is the greatest iniury that can be against the law of *hospitalitie.* This law (we read) was so religiously observed of Antiquitie, that had anie one come vnder their roofe (though he were their mortal enemy) yet dared they do no other, but entertaine him with faire language, and send him away with safe conduct. And hence it was that [c] *Themistocles* being banished from Athens, and pursued by the Athenians, was forced to flie for rescue vnto the house of that citizen, who had ever beene his mortal enemy, & at that present the present cause of his banishment. Whereinto neverthelesse being entered, he was curteously receiued, and delivered foorth in friendly manner. Should then a Christian deale more roughly with his wife, then the heathē would with their enimy? Surely the world wil condemne vs for men of litle wisedome, or els it would neuer haue commended them for their laudable custome.

Arist ibi-
dem.

Let

Let me ioine vnto Aristotle a follower of his, a worthy philosopher and famous [a] Doctor: whose opinion is, that wiues are to be perswaded by reason, not cōpelled by authoritie: led on by perswasion, not drawne by cōpulsion, induced by lenity, not cōstrained by seueritie. For they are one flesh, one minde togither with vs: howbeit then this minde bee troubled with perturbations, and this flesh be wounded with affections, yet should we seeke some cordial to heale them, not a Corrosiue to afflict thē, for by afflicting them we afflict our selues. But to passe this easier combat, & to enter the lists with you in your owne schoole, giue me leaue to aske counsell of the *Law* in this case.

[a] Vir ornat. D.Dr. Casus in Comment. suis in hūc locum.

Chapt. 4.

The same discussed by the Civill and Canon law.

And as the law in general is generally held the groūd-work & foūdatiō of a cōmō-wealth, in whose bosome iustice is seated the sole preseruer of good gouernement: so the *Canon* and *Civill* of al other the *species* are by most approued (yet how iustlie I cannot tel) the chiefest formes thereof. Whether it bee for its largenesse and vniversalitie, because obserued in almost al our christian world: or for its plainenesse and perspicuitie, because applied wel neare to each particular case of each seueral estate. Neverthelesse in these also by my slender obseruation I haue found a certaine kinde of ſtrickneſſe and obduritie, againſt no condition more then againſt the eſtate of wiues. For inſtance.[b] It decrees, a wife ſhal looſe her dowrie for giving a laſcivious kiſſe.[c] That a wife is legally boūd to follow her huſband wandring at his pleaſure from citty to citty.[d] Be it, from one land into another region.[e] Be it, frō her owne country into baniſhmēt it ſelf.[f] Eſpecially if it be in pilgrimage vnto the holy land.[g] That the wife is onlie dignified by the huſband, and not any waies the huſband graced by the wife.[h] That the huſbands ſuſpition of his wifes lightnes may bee the wiues expulſion from her huſbands company. Laſtly, if a[i] wife play the Adultereſſe (a fault indeed deſerving no excuſe,) her huſband may then produce her into publike iudgment, depriue her of her promiſed dowry and expoſe her to perpetual divorcement.[k] But if the huſbād cōmit the like offence, though it were as open as the ſun, & as odious as hate it ſelfe, yet the wife may not in publike as much as open her mouth againſt it. Infinite ſuch other. Hard impoſitions in my weake ſenſe for ſo weake a ſexe. And ſuch alſo as long ſince haue beene deplored by *Syra* in the Comedian

[a] *Alas we women liue in ſervile awe,*
But men inioie a freedome of the lawe.
For if a huſband ſerue in Venus pay
Apparantly, the wife muſt nothing ſaie.
Yet if a wife chance ſteale her wantonneſſe,
The law is open for the mans redreſſe.

[b] Auth. cōſt. Neop. lib. 3 rubrica. 46. Idem. Aur. quæſt. per Io. Acar q. 34 nu. 2.
[c] Iaſon in l. de Att. ff. Idem Duacon. in tit. ſoluto matrimonio.
[d] Petr. de Ancha. ſuper decret in c. num. 16.
[e] Alcit. t a.
[f] D. Aloyſius. de le. in l. 5. ad L. Iul. v. l 4.
[g] Com op. lib. 5. tit. de nupt. 2.
[h] Decis Vivij. lib. 2. deci. 241. nu 4
[i] Bald. & Ang. Aret in L. imp. ff. de ſtatu hominis.
[k] Cod. lib 9 co 7. ad le. Iul. de adul & ſtupr.
[a] Tranſl. ex Plauto in Com. Mer.

Ecaſtor (inquit) lege dura vivūt mulieres. Multoq; inquiore miſeræ, quā viri, &c.

But

But were the lawes equall to both the same,
VVe soone should see who most deserueth blame.

If the adultery of a wife be a wrong vnto the husband, why not the adultery of an husband an iniury vnto the wife? Or if suspitiō only may discharge a man of his wife, who is more happy thē the iealous husband, who as often as his minde changeth may therwithal change his wife? Or if al the lustre and glory of wedlocke descend only from the husband vnto the wife, and none reflexe againe from the wife vnto the husband, it is hard to be conceived how there cā be a true society, or a fit match? The like may be said of the rest. But al are so palpably against reason, that there is no reasonable mā who wil seeme to reason for them.

Nowe the rigour & severity of these & the like laws against womē, are supposed by [b] some to haue proceeded from the lawgivers, not hate but ignorance. Who for the most part (altogither the Canonists) being single and vnmarried mē, knew not so wel the estate and mysterie of marriage. And so conceiving perchance no better of a wife, then as a mans best servant, ranked thē in a degree of two low servility. Neither is their reason vnprobable. For who can discerne the suns brightnes that never sawe the light? Who can iudge of a pure scarlet who never was acquainted with difference of colours? who cā giue a true cēsure in schollership, who never was so much as baptized at the Muses font? Right so who cā rightly estimate the rites of marriage, who never knew the happines thereof?

[b] Vide Tyraquillum de legibus connub.

But I accuse not the law: for these former positions are for the most parte but deductions from thence. Neither reprehend I these Law-givers; for they were ancient trophees of yet living glory. Yet needs must I finde some fault with some Interpreters of the law, who fit the square vnto the timber, not the timber vnto the square: working the law as a waxen nose hither and thither, as the tide & tempest of their braine-sicke fancie driues them. Which no where is more apparently seene, then in the case we haue now in hand. For in the whole body of either Law, Canō or Civil, I haue not yet found (neither, as I thinke, hath any man els) set downe in these or equivalent termes, or otherwise past by any positiue sentence or verdit *That it is lawfull for a husbande to beate his wife.* But whatsoever is cited thēce are either far fetcht conclusions, or vnfriendly sequels, which hang as wel togither being toucht in iudicious trial, as the ioints of a rotten carcasse engibbited, being tossed with a violent winde.

There being nothing then directly against vs in the substance of the law, let vs see what the shadowes thereof I meane the Interpreters please to determine. Whose opinions I finde as various, as they make the subiect of their opinion vncōstant. And therefore I must place them in their severall rankes.

In the first such * who peremptorily hold it lawful. But finding themselues orepreſt with contrary reasons; as men altogither desperate vse such tur-

* Glos. in l. & si quemcunque pa rag. vl. in fi. ff. ad l. Aqu.

nings

nings and windings; such evasions, and contradictions; such poore shifts and trivial sophismes, as the learned may wel laugh at, the ignoraunt perchance admire. If you haue seene a mill-horse passing his circle, or a spannel turning round after his taile, you may iustly conceiue how those mē tread the maze of their vncertaine opinion. Some of them, and amongst this bad the best: hold it lawful but not convenient. Sillie men, not knowing that good lawes are never the direct authors of inconvenience. Some a little more frondicke then the first, thinke it lawful & convenient too, but it must bee but a little forsooth, slightly, and but seldome. Having indeed forgottē, or els hauing never learned, that circumstances can but lessen a fault, never of an action absolutly evil cōvert it into good. Some other there are the overgrowne monsters of tiranie, who proclaime it frō out the top of folie; That a husband may beate his wife much or litle according to his pleasure, and as the occasiō is. Nay more that he may publikely shame her, and if he lists imprison her too. Mē who seeme to haue banished al humanity; of an yron hart; of a brasen brow, and both so cankered with vice, that vertue can get no impression. For what is it that letteth loose the raines vnto furie, and giues madnesse its whole scope? What is it that violats the holy rites of marriage? What is it that infringeth the sacred bonds of loue? What is it that breeds horride and domestical massakers? What is that abolisheth all vertuous and matrimonial societie, if this do not?

Alb. Grand in tract ma l. fic. tit. de pæ. reo. col vlt.
Lucas Pen in lib quicunq; Col. 2. & 3. C de Mil. lib 12.
lo And. & Panor. in d c lit ille col 2. in v. incertis. hic col. penul vers.
A. Aurex quæst lib 3 quæst. 18. nu 9. & 10.
Alexander Consil 113 Col. 1. & 2. v. 3.
Bald. Consil. 176.
Bouhic. super 2 decr. de jure iurando.
Plures si velis quore A Taraquellam. de legib. connubial. in gl. 1.

Jn the second ranke are those, [b] who out of a staid iudgment and vpright minde, hold it not onely vnlawful, but an odious, vnmanly, and vnseemelie thing. Odious in respect of the breach of their faith given in wedlocke. Vnmanly in regarde of woman weaknesse, and imbecillitie. Vnseemely for examples sake. And therefore in consideration of all is altogither vnlawfull. Learned & vertuous men

VVhose praise the sacred Goddesse of eternitie
[a] Keepes hallowed in the eternall shryne of fame:
Vertue doth build them trophees: Dignitie
Crownes their desert; & waites vpō their name.
And worthy are they of a marble stone,
Made blessed by an Homers pen, or none.

Jn the third are such, [b] who though they haue writ ten whole tractes and large volumes concerning the estate of wiues, of their dowries, of their inheritance, of their portions, of their vows, of their diuorcements, and like infinite circumstances. Yet haue not a word of this question, nor vouchsafe to grace it with a graceful terme. Perchance because they thought it so hainous & ougly a paradoxe as vnfit to be matched with so many honest & goodly precepts of the law; or els so vile a position as vnworthy to be affirmed by a Lawyer.

These are the opinions. So disagreeing you see and altogither contrary, that whosoever waigheth them in the true scales of an vpright iudgmēt, can by them, but hardly rest satisfied in them. For

[b] Donellus de iure civili l. 13. c. 21. Decianus. leg. 9. c. 11. num. 17. And. Tyraquillus de legib. connub aureū opus. Anchar. Consl. 408. n. 3. Iason. Luppus Angelus Aretinus plerique alij. Tar. vid gl 1. de leg. con.

[a] Transl è Sta. vbi incip Quorū sacra tenet sacris redimita, &c.

[b] Bursatus, eq. aur. imperialis aulæ Con. Palestin. in mag. op. Guido a Bayso. Val Fost. Barbat. Bolognet. D. de Rota Decius, & maxima sane pars in vtroque jure periti.

where

where trueth seemeth to haue taken vp her seate, there authority disguiseth her; and where she cannot be found there fancie would needs discrie her. Everie man making an Idol of his owne conceite, and partially impairing an other mans iudgment. Not finding therefore in them the certainety wee seeke for: let vs compare reason vnto reason, oppose Lawyer vnto Lawyer, conferre opinion with opinion. And drawing frō the law it selfe certaine grounds and foundations in this point, by the ful clearing of them, we shal giue a faire light vnto our intended purpose.

My first ground shalbe the [c] superiority of husbandes over their wiues: wherevnto answereth the [d] reverence of wiues towardes their husbandes. This superioritie appeareth first in the manner of their first wedlocke, wherein the woman was made [e] of man, and [f] for man, and given in tuition by God [g] vnto man. Secondly in the difference of their sexe, because *Nature*, and the God of *Nature* in everie kinde hath given preheminēce vnto the male. Thirdly in mans vniversal soveraignetie, which he receiued ouer al creatures [h] when God installed him his vice-roy ouer all the world. And howsoeuer it was not so absolute a prerogatiue in regard of his fellow woman, as it was in respect of others, because she was ioin'd in commission with him. [i] Yet such it was as might wel beare the title of superioritie for the man: and of the woman require a duty of reverence. But neither is the one so predominant, nor the o-

[c] Cod. li. 6. tit 40 lege 5. & plerisq. alijs locis.
[d] Ibidem: subsequent. verbis.
[e] Gen. 2. 22
[f] Gen. 2. 20
[g] Gen. 2. 23
[h] Gen. 1. 28
[i] S. Chrysost. hom. 9. in Gen. Ruper. li. 2. de Trinitate.

ther so servile, as that from them should proceede any other fruits but of a roial protection, and loial subiection.

My second ground shalbe the [k] power or commande of husbands over their wiues: [a] whereunto answeareth the obedience of wiues towards their husbands. And here I neede not to wearie out my pen, in deciding the cõtroversies touching the authoritie of husbands cõcerning their wiues goods: possessions, lands, dowries and the like. Only pertaining to my purpose is the commãde over their persons. Which the law [b] determines to consist, partely in imposing on them convenient labours for the supportance of their estate; chiefly in exacting the rightes of marriage for the procreation of children, and avoidance of lust. To the former as much as in her lieth the wife must yeeld obedience. To the latter (vnlesse on some [c] restrictions which modesty refers vnto my margẽts) she is legally bound to giue contentment. Neverthelesse in both, harde it is to bee iudged whether the husband should commande with greater obeysance, or the wife obey with greater commande. Both so vnitely strife to expresse the effects of so perfit a vnion: both so interchangeably labour for the building vp of the *Temple* of *loue*.

My third ground shalbe, [d] The correction lawfully vsed by husbands against their wiues; where-

[k] Digest. li. 38. tit. 1. lege. 48. Cod. loco superius citato. & Inst 2. Inst. 2.

[a] Ibidem. vt iure etiam Bald in C. 1 tit. An mariti suc. vxor.

[b] Ang. Aretin. Inst. d. S. C. Bar. in d. li. j. parag. j. ff. de iniur: & cæteri.

[c] Viz. In tempore menstr. prægnãtiæ. Immũditiæ ægritudinis Infantiæ. sacræ abstinentiæ. Vti habet. Pau Ca. in d l. rei jud. iuncta l seq ff. Anto. a Prat. & alij

[d] Gl. in leg si quécũq; parag. vl. in fi. ff. ad L. Aquil. Gl. in auth. vt lic. matr: & aviæ parag. Quia vero quædam mulieres in ver. sufficere, Cæteri, vide Tiraquil. 2. lib. Connub. gl. 2. parte. 2.

vnto

vnto answereth the [f] submission required of wiues vnto their husbands. This correction being a punishment, must (according to the rule of law) bee proportioned unto the fault punished. The faults of wiues towards their husbands, are al comprised vnder three several degrees; and therefore the punishments likewise must be of three several sorts.

f ibidem.

In the first and highest degree are faults altogither vnexcusable, neuer committed by anie vertuous or modest wife: never endured by anie loving or honest husbād. Such are the defiling of his marriage bed: or against his life & person any trecherous exploite. For these the law sets downe direct punishments. For the former [g] divorce from the bond of marriage: for the second [h] expulsion from the community of wedlocke. And in neither case are the husbands ingaged for paymēt of their dowry, or any waies bound for reliefe of their poverty. Mistake me not. I only intend that the prosequution hereof lieth in the husbands power not the execution. For that must be consummate in lawful manner: the fact proved by lawful witnesse: the verdit given by a lawful iudge. So that the iealousie of husbandes touching their wiues incontinencie, or suspition otherwise concerning their disloialty, before they come into actual proofe are no actual faults of the wife, but to be adiudged as the braine-sicke fancies of their fond husbands. Be the suspition of the one vehement, it beareth indeed the better colour, and deserveth the sharper trial. But for the iealosie of the other it is a com-

g Reg glos TVæ de procurato. Cod. lib 9. ad l Iul. de adul. & stupr.

h Syntagma cómunium opin. vide. l. 7. 52. n. 23.

mon

mon ill humour', and therefore in 'wiſedome nothing at all to bee eſteemed. Jealouſie is a childe conceived of ſelfe-vnworthines, and of anothers worth, at whoſe birth feare made it an abortiue in nature, and a monſter in loue. For the iealous man vnworthily loving a worthily beloved obiect, ſtãds in feare of cõmunicating his good, vnto an other more worthy. So that neither is his loue perfit, becauſe mixt with feare which loue abhorreth, nor his feare medicinable, becauſe conioind with loue which feare impoiſoneth. But of both ariſeth this *mungrel* kinde of iealouſie, a loving feare, or a fearfull loue. Wherein (contrary to al other actions of man) we bend al our diligence, and carefulneſſe to obtaine the full ſight and perfit aſſuraunce of our owne miſery. We would needs forſooth, know our ſelues to be ſuch Becoes, as we feare to be. For of prevention there is no hope. Our Engliſh worthie can tell vs.

[a] S. Phil. Sydn. Arc. lib 3.

[a] *Sure tis no iealouſie can that prevent,*
VVhereto two perſons once be full content.

Being then that theſe imaginations of huſbandes, are not in law the faults of a wife: and when it chãceth that ſuch great faults are, they are determined of their lawful puniſhmẽts: whatſoever other correctiõs are added in this caſe, are done beſides the law.

Jn the ſecond degree are faultes of another nature, farre inferiour to the former, and yet of ſome moment alſo. Such may be their backwardneſſe in the religious ſervice of God. Careleſneſſe in mannaging

naging

naging their houſhold-affaires: Jll behaviour towards their neighbours and friends: milde mainour in regard of themſelues and huſbands. Theſe I cõfeſſe to be as ſo many rootes of weede planted in the faire garden-plot of a womans minde; ſpreading into many crooked brãches & bearing much bitter fruit. In [b] theſe therfore the law alloweth huſbands to vſe reprehenſion either ſharper or milder, according as the qualitie of the fault requireth and as their owne modeſt diſcretion findeth convenience. Yet neverthe leſſe theſe faults are not ſo abſolutely evill, but that they might admit ſome kinde of excuſe: Inſomuch as they may therby be ſomewhat extenuated, though perchãce not peremptorily defended.

[b] Tex. in parag necesse est 47 dist & facis C. indignã tur in fine. 32. q. 6. Glos. in l. si quemcunqꝫ parag. vl. in f. ff. ad l. Aquil. Tyraquil i. l. con. gl. 1. par. 1.

For the firſt, there is no man ſo irreligious, but commends a religious woman: eſpecially a religious wife, in whom religion is eſpecially needfull, both for inſtruction of her family and education of her children. But if in ſuch, an imagination of religion fal into ſome peeviſh zeale through ignorance, or through ſome ſmal meaſure of knowledge amount vnto a womanniſh reſolution; it had beene better they had been leſſe ſtudious in thoſe pointes, where the beſt fruit of their labours is a plentiful ſheiſe of errours. Wherfore for my part I could never approue thoſe too too holy womẽgoſpellers, who weare their teſtament at their apron-ſtrings, and wil weekely catechize their huſbands, citing places, clearing difficulties, & preaching holy ſermons too, if the ſpirit of their devotion moue them. For ſure I am, antiquity helde ſilence to be a womās chiefeſt eloquēce, & thought it their part to heare more thē to ſpeake, to learne rather then to teach. Alſwel then too much curioſitie of religion, as too much neglect is a fault in women. So that if their frailty lead thē into either extreame, the huſband hath the bit of reprehenſiō in his power to keepe them in the golden maine.

Againe if a wife be over frugall, it may bee ſuppoſed it is for the augmenting of her huſbandes eſtate, and benefit of his children. If ſhee be very bountiful, it may be thought ſhe intends her huſbandes credit, and ſupportance of his eſtimation. Likewiſe if others miſlike her carriage, it maie bee her modeſty ſeemeth pride vnto them, or her familiaritie otherwiſe breedeth contempt. Laſtlie if through infirmity ſhe fal into any inconvenience, ſome things are to be given to the weaknes of her ſexe, ſome matter of excuſe there is in the rarenes of ſuch offence. In al or either of theſe aggreivances, the huſbād hath alwaies the raines in his own directiō. And what more ſoveraigne medicine, thē a huſbands tender reprehenſion? What is there that can more effectually moue then a word from his mouth? What ſooner inforce alleagance then a frowne of his countenance?

In the laſt and loweſt degree are ſome ſmal and trivial faults. Indeed vertues in their owne nature, but in their practiſe perchance are tainted with ſome ſavour of vice. Such may be the nimbleneſſe of womens tongues, which although may ſometimes be imploied to their husbands disturbance, yet for the most part are busied in their good. In marchandizing for their profit, in refreshing their wearied spirites, ofttimes in entertaining their friends with curteous complement: commonly in the vsual performance of other such offices, as vsually belong to such a quality. Of this sort likewise are womens affected curiositie of apparel: their over-nice standing on preheminence: their womanish dislikings, and their fond longings, with other such slender errours; obliquities rather of nature, then faults in manners. Al which a husband might easily reforme, either in his wisdome not stouping so low, as to take notice of them, or from out his loue mildly to touch them. Howsoeuer, his allowance in these points is only [a] admonition. Which as it is the fairest kinde of correction, so it taketh the best effect in any good nature. You know that many sorts of soft waters will pierce deeper then the dint of hardest steele. And many thinges by mildnes haue bin accomplished, which through violence could never. Pollicy goeth beyond force in martial actions; wisedome beyond rigour in domestical affaires. And [b] far safer is the obedience yeelded vp on faire termes, then that which is cōstrained on foule conditions: for the one proceeds from loue, & is even filiall, the other commeth of feare, and is only servile.

[a] Iurisconsl. in l. vlt. ff. si quis aliq. test prohib S. Bernard in ep. ad Raymund. de re fam. Vide Tyraq. 1. l. cōnub. gl. 1. par. 1.

[b] Plutarch. in prec cōnubialibus.

Now that there cannot be thought any misdemainour of a wife towards her husband, not comprised vnder one of these three, is by discourse plainly manifest. And that there ought not to bee vsed by a husband towards his wife any other correction besides these three shal evidētly be proved

Concerning the former. Our haters of women haue indeede well imitated the olde Tragedians, whose vse it was, when they would set forth anie odious scene, to plucke the eares of their auditors downe into hell, to invocate the furies, to muster vp cursed spirits, and whatsoever was most ougly to the eie of their vnderstanding: to the end they might make their expression more vehement, & leaue a deeper impression behinde thē. They likewise are well skill'd in this excellent art of railing. They coniure vp whole catalogues of vices, they number out numberlesse obliquities, and rake togither as many sins as the world is guilty of: fastning them on women, as on the authors & actors of them al. Pride *(say they) and greater then an other pride, the pride of selfe-worth in vnworthinesse: Avarice, anger, luxury, gluttonie, slouthfulnesse, envy, are the vsual inhabitants of a womans minde. It much offendeth not, that they are vngrateful to their friends, impatient in their coller, babblers of their tongue, witty in their deceipts, wilful in their resolutions, ambitions, flattering, lustful, dissembling: but that they will needes also proue, the cut-throats of friendship, & yet seeme to be our friends. A punishment for man, and yet an ineuitable punishment: a tētatiō of man and yet a natural tentation: a calamitie to man, and yet a desired calamitie: an absolute, and yet a necessa-

* Myogynes quidam cuius totā spurcam & impuram declamationem recitat Tyraq. 1.1 con gl. 3. par. 1.

rie

rie evil. Infinit are their reproaches. And I ſhould forget the nature of an apology, if I ſpake any farther in their foule language.

First then let mee giue theſe *Cynickes* to vnderſtand, that their trade is not now ſo good as they could wiſh it were: for their chiefe ware *detraction* is helde but for childrens rhetoricke. And *Invectiues* are counted the pooreſt ſhare in learning. They are but the froath of an apiſh invention: the purge of an idle braine; the falling-ſicknes of a giddy wit, flat hereſies in true ſchollerſhip. For when you haue ſpoken al that malice can ſpeake againſt woman, what yet haue you ſpokē that may not be applied vnto mē? Sin (you may remēber) is of the neuter gender, and therefore neither hateth the one ſexe, nor cleaveth vnto the other, but is too familiarly acquainted with both maſculine and fœminine. Was *Lais* a whore? ſhe was but one: many men in Athens were her minions; but I ſtraine not the compariſon.

All women (you ſaie) are altogither evil: of men you are ſure there are ſome good. And are they evil all? Why, then (ô graue [a] *Plutarch*) how came it to paſſe thy wiſdome ſo failed thee? ancient [b] *Heſiode*, who corrupted thy mature iudgement? [c] *Cælius* who beguiled thy wit? [d] *Chaucer*, how miſcaried thy golden pen? Learned and moſt holy Saints, [e] *S. Hierom*, [f] *S. Gregory*, [g] *S. Cypriā*, *S. Chryſoſtome*, who deceived you al? for deceived you al are (if this poſitiō be received) who haue ſeverally writtē ſeveral tracts in honor of honorable womē. Are they al

[a] Plutarch. lib. de clar. fœm.
[b] Heſiodus lib. de mulier. heroid
[c] Cælius li. lection. antiquarum.
[d] Chaucer. lib. fæminarum encomion. 1. & alterum, de laudib. bonarum fæminar.
[e] S. Greg. Syntagm. de muſis.
[g] S. Cyprian. lib de ſingularitate fæminarum
[h] S. Chryſoſtom. in hom. decollat. Io. Baptiſtæ.

evil?How came the whole world then to be so be-sotted, as to recorde a famous memorie of manie millions of them? Of Cannonized Saints, of con-stant Martyrs, of graue matrons, of chast virgins, of most vertuous and vnspotted wiues? Neither are such as I speake of *Phœnices*, rare and but sel-dome found. Search all histories; travell with the sun round about the earth; recall the former daies even from the worlds minority, & compare them with the latter times vnto this present age; you shal finde that the nūber of vertuous women may wel equallize the number of men that haue beene vertuous. And howbeit I cannot say that there is any womā such an absolute paragō of vertue, who is voide of al vice: *Venus* had her mole, the brigh-test sun suffers an eclipse, the purest golde is not without some drosse, nor the best of women free from al reproofe. Yet thus I say, to obiect all vices whatsoeuer haue been in al women in general, vn-to every woman in particular, is most iniurious. Were such a conclusiō of any force, I would thus dispute. *Catiline* was a Traitor; *Verres* a thiefe; *Ne-ro* a murderer; *Ægistus* an adulterer; *Machivell* atheistical; *Iovianus* heretical; *Battus* a foole, o-thers, other such. These all were men *Misogynes* is a man; therefore *Mysogynes* is a traitor, a thiefe, a murderer, an adulterer, hee is atheistical, hee is heretical, he is a foole, or what els you please. The forme of argumentatiō is your owne. Which if you dislike, you cleare women of whatsoever is here spoken against them: If approue, you haue al this while travelled with the *Pellican*, & the birth of your owne childe, wil be your own (if not distru-ction) yet discredit.

By this time perchãce your heat is qualified, & you think thẽ not as before you did *absolute evils*: but refining your phrase terme thẽ in the last edition [i] *Necessary evils*. This indeed is the cõmon tenure, and most men thinke they haue iudiciouslie spoken, whẽ thus they haue defined the case. That they are necessarie therefore I wil easilie graunt, since hee that made man saw it was not good that man should be without them. That they are evils I vtterly deny, since he that made woman sawe that al he made was good. Js woman good then in the iudgement of God, and in your conceit also necessarie? then once againe you must alter your stile & hence forth write her a *Necessary good*. For these very termes *Necessary* and *evill* are incompetent, they are at dissention amongst themselues, they cannot stand peaceably togither. All things that are necessary for man are good; food is necessarie, it is good. Apparel necessary, it is good. The fire, the aire, the earth, the water necessary, they are good: women necessary, and therefore good. For els if wee suppose that God hath bound man in so hard a condition, that some thinges are left necessarie for him, yet evil, we both impaire the wisdom of God, and detract from his goodnesse. But to satisfie some chiefe authours of this received opinion: I answere that some women are lesse good thẽ other and thence they incurre the name of evill: &

[i] Quod vetus apud Græcos proverb. ἀναγκαῖον κακόν.

nar-

nature requiring a necessity of them, thence they receiue that title of necessarie: & from both they are branded with the infamie of *Necessarie evils*. An attribute yet not appropriat vnto them, but vsually also applied vnto men.[a] *Alexander Severus* an Emperour of *Rome*, called his counsellours necessarie evils: his provincials necessary evils; the officers in his court necessary evils. [b] *Hybicus* in like sort called *Euthidamus* his friend his necessary evil. [c] *Varro* his testie brother his necessarie evill, [d] *Martiall* his angry companion his necessarie evill. With whom (saith he) I can neither liue wel, nor yet liue without him.

[a] Vita de eo` narrat Aelius Lampidius.
[b] Stra. l. 14.
[c] Varro.
[d] Martial. de seipsis narrant.

But to break of this idle cavillation, which hath too long withhelde me from my purposed course. Let *Mysogynes* steepe his quill in the gall of Invection, let him speak with as open a mouth as ever Satyre did; yet al that can be alleadged, as offences of wiues against their husbands, are only such as either are expressly mentioned, or els directly may be reduced vnto my three former heads.

Secondly then that the corrections lawfully vsed by a husband vnto his wife, ought to be no other then I haue prescribed, remaines as yet to be more amply proued. For the first, that *divorcemēts* in cases prefixed are the sole & only lawful punishment, the law it selfe affords so faire testimonies, & the practise of all Lawyers hethervnto haue given so ful confirmation, that now it is too late either to be denied, or gaine-said. For the two other *M. Aurelius* a Consull sometimes and Councellour

shall

shal speake for me. *A wife (saith he) is often to be admonished, to be reprehended but seldome, never to be dealt withal with violent handes.* Where you see not only a flat denial of any rigorous sort of correcting wiues; but withall a plaine assertion of my prescribed punishmentes, *admonition* and *reprehension.*

Admonition it is, that with a tender hande bendeth vp the wound of a friend, and therefore most needful in marriage the nearest of any friendship. Hẽce the[c] law inioines vs to deale with our wiues in milde termes, in loving talke, in gentle and faire speech. That whereas by nature womẽ are milde, loving, gentle & faire, they might not choose but best accept that frõ others, which is most like vnto themselues. *Mercurie* (saith [a] *Plutarch*) was seated the next God vnto *Venus*, because in marriage there is alwaies neede of settled reason, and a faire language: *Mars* was then vshering of *Iupiter* in a place remote, because that warres are only fit for kings and states.

[c] Iuriscons. in l. vlt. ff. si quis aliq. test. proh.

[a] Plut. li. de praec. connub.

Reprehension we haue added in the secõd place, that where admonition with its smooth carriage prevailed not, there reprehension with sharper intreaty might take effect. Hence the [b] law councelleth that overmuch lenity is to be mixt with some few graines of severity, and of thẽ both to be made a third temperature, or golden compound, called Mediocritie. By which in al our reproofes we shal be so guided, as neither vsing too much exasperation or indulgence, we may soone reforme what-

[b] Vide Tyraquil. 1. li. connub. gl. 1. par. 1. & Greg. M. Moral. lib. 20 par. 20. par. 4. c. 11.

 soever

soever offence. God commaunded that in the Arke of the *Tabernacle*, directly over his two *Statute-tables* should be *Mana* preserved, but togither with *Moses* rodde. [d] Papirius set vp before the Senate house in *Rome* the image of *Mercie*, but placed *Iustice* therewithal. *Iupiter*

[d] Liv. vide l. 8. hist. ab vrb. cond. Ovid. Met. lib. 2.

[e] Blanditijs precibusq; minas regaliter addit.

> [e] *To his intreatie, and his faire perswasion,*
> *Adioined threatnings in his princely fashion,*

What God himselfe prescribed in matters legall, *Papirius* in civil, *Iupiter* in Imperial: the like maie we likwise follow in mannaging of domestical and vxorial affaires. If the Manna allured not, the rod should cōstraine; if commiseration prevailed not; iustice shoulde succeede, if praiers were reiected, threatnings should terrifie; and if an husbands admonitions be not esteemed, his reprehension thē should not be spared.

In both which kinds of correction our successe shalbe the farre more effectual, if we lead the waie before by our example, which by our wordes wee perswade our wiues to follow. For the abbreviarie of an husbands words and actions, is as it were the chamber-glasse whereby a wife shoulde addresse her selfe. At his tongue she should learne to speak, by his carriage she should compose her behavior. And a thousand times safer way it is (as in a case not much different [f] *Pacatus* told *Theodosius*.) to governe by example, thē by severity. Every good example is a most pleasing inuitation vnto vertue, where the eie is guided vnto present action, not the eare fed with fained speculatiō. And herevpon

[f] Vide Tytaq loco supr. citato

was

was [g] *Petrarch* his opinion grounded, that a mimical husband wil make a lascivious wife, a riotous husband a voluptuous wife, a prowde husband a prowde wife, a modest and honest husband a modest and honest wife. Wherefore it is [h] S. *Austens* counsel, that such as we woulde haue our wiues appeare vnto vs, the same wee shoulde first approue our selues vnto them. Would wee haue thē chast of their bodie, civil in their carriage, pure & vnspotted of the world? we thē must walke before them as the patternes of chastitie, of civillitie, of irreprehensiō. For what reason haue we to expect more of them, then we cā performe of our selues? Jt is a silly master that offendeth in those faults, for which he is offended with his pupil. So is it an impudent and impious fellow (saith [i] *Seneca*) who of his wife requireth an vndefiled bed, yet he himselfe defiles it. By our vertuous demainour then wee must direct thē in the way of vertue; for there are none of them vicious who wil sticke to tel vs that we are their masters. Jt is reported by [k] esteemed authors, that in some places the husbands are punished only for the faults of their wiues. Jn *Catalonia*, whosoever is cuckoled paieth a summe of mony: in *Parrice* he rideth in disgrace through the citty, the crier proclaiming these wordes before him, *so do, so haue*. In some parts of England I haue seene a custome not much different. All which though they now are wel neare worne out of date, yet their primary intent was vertuous, being to restraine husbandes to the loving and living with

[g] Petrarch. lib. de rem. adver. fort.

[h] S. Aug. in C. si dictum 23. q. 6.

[i] Senec. ad Lucil. epist. 94.

[k] Guil. de Monte laud. in Cl. cum ex eo. Cardinal. Flor m. I. oppo. de sent. exon.

their owne wiues, so that neither should need any other company, but by their mutual example one should bee a president vnto the other of true chastitie.

Thus then (to draw my selfe vnto an end) & only thus may an husband lawfully correct his wife. *Admonitiō* is his first degree for smallest faults; this must proceed from a patient loue, or a louing patience. The next is *reprehension* in greater offences; this must aime at the amendment of the fault, not offending of the faulty. Both of these must bee seconded by our good example, that the worlde may see vs do those things which wee would haue done by others. Lastly in the last & highest degree is *Divorce* in such cases as before are alleadged. Now for farther satisfactiō, to proue that the laws allowe not any verberall correction I haue added these few reasons.

First. If a husband may lawfully beate his wife, then is the wife legally bounde to indure his beating. For the lawe giues not authoritie to the punisher, but therewithal inioines obedience on the punished. But the lawe bindes not a wife to such blockish patience. For in such a case it [c] allows her to depart from her husband; [d] and of her husbande in time of her absence to obtaine sufficient mainetenaunce. [e] Neither doeth it limitte her anie time to returne if shee feare his tyrannie: nor yet [f] constraines her to liue againe with him, vnlesse for her good vsage bee giuen her good securitie.

[c] Vide Aegidium in curia Par. Prael. v. 2. q 195. n. 7.
[d] Vincen. de Franc. decis. 144. n. 4.
[e] Petr. de Ferrar in aur pr p. 424. n. 4.
[f] Durandus in spec. juris, lib. 1, de off. iud, parag. 2, n. 8.

Jn answere whereof that shift will not serue, to saie the *Law* authorizeth a man to beate his wife but slightlie, and not in such sorte as may cause her departure. This is too course a salue for such a soare. For a little beating vnto some women, is more then much vnto others; and therefore in them it wil breede the same or worse effectes: & how little so euer it bee they are not bound to take it.

Secondlie [g] the lawe decrees that he lesse grieuouslie offendeth who killeth his mother, then he who killeth his wife, though both be most hainous and execrable sinnes. Hence by rule of disputation I conclude, therefore also hee lesse grieuouslie offendeth that beates his mother, then hee who beates his wife. But what a horride and barbarous fact it is for a man to beate his mother iudge you, & then also iudge what the other is which is worse then that.

[g] S. Bonavent lib. 4. dist. 38. art. 2. quest. 2.

And whatsoever is saide amongst Lawyers of the first proposition, some plainelie affirming it, others mincing it with distinction, auaileth nothing. For if (as manie doe) you holde the offence onlie greater in respect of the greater punishment allotted it by the law, but lesse in it selfe, and of his owne nature: I would demaunde you whether the lawe doe not proportionate everie punishment to the qualitie of everie offence? To smal offences light punishmẽts; to the greater, punishmẽts of greater torture; to those that are most hainous most exquisite torments? Which if you grant you must necessarily acknowledge the truth of the first proposition: if you deny you accuse the law of iniustice. Or otherwise if your reply be (as most mens is) that herein the law was especiallie heedful: and because mē are more prone to iniure their wiues then their parents (as lamentable accidents most vsually do testifie) therfore for greater terrour to such offenders, & more evident example to other spectators, the law more severely punished the one then the other. If thus you pleade I then ioine hands with you: & in the present case giue the same sentence. Because men are more prone to beat their wiues then their parents, therfore in law the act should bee held more hainous, because by lawe the punishmente must bee more greivous.

Thirdly the name of a wife is a name of dignity: The law stiles her thy familiar friend: thine equal associate: the Mistresse of thy house: to speake at once, the same person and *Individuum* (as it were) togither with thee. If therfore she beare the name of dignity, shee is to be respected: If thy familiar friend shee is to be imbraced: if thy equal associat, shee is equally to be regarded: If thy Mistresse, she is to be honoured: if thy verie selfe, shee is dearelie to be beloued. All which duties of an husband are necessarily intended by the law; and are as contrarie to the rough and vnkinde vsage of a wife, as fire vnto water, heaven vnto earth.

And for the mittigation which is here by some men interposed in way of answere vnto this obiection:(which is, that in the ſtrickneſſe of law, for a huſband to beate his wife is lawful, but it is vnconvenient in the decencie of manners:) It is a plaine and peeviſh contradiction, & iniuriouſly robbeth the law of the end of the law. For the end of the law is the happy government of a cõmon-wealth which happineſſe is in nothing more eminentlie ſeene then in the decent conformitie of manners, and orderly behaviour in al eſtates. And hence it is that the Lawyer as a laborious travellour goeth through al eſtates, to bring al vnto decencie. Hee ordereth the eſtate of Monarches and princes: of peires and nobles: of Magiſtrates and ſubiectes: of parents and children, of huſbands & wiues: of Maſters and ſervants. [c] And in the whole body of a common-weale whatſoever is out of decent temper muſt by the law be ordered, as a ſicke part in a body natural by phyſicke cured. So that then an abſolute *indecorum* in manners (as they confeſſe the beating of a wife to be) is an abſolute breach of the law.

[c] Plat lib. 1. de iuſto. finem legis dicit cõvenientem ſervare ordinem, odiſſe mala.

Laſtly correctiõ by way of beating (ſay the beſt you can ſay of it) is meerely ſervile: and in manie mens iudgements ſo inhumane, as that a wiſe man whoſe actions flow frõ diſcreet premeditatiõ, will not exerciſe it vpon his ſlaues or ſwaines. But ſervilitie is only to be impoſed on ſuch as are ſervile; and therefore not on wiues who are in the law free burgeſſes of the ſame citie whereof their huſbands are free, and free deniſons in the ſame land wherin their huſbandes are free: both participating the ſame rightes, both inioying the ſame liberties.

But here againe ariſeth a cavil touching the precepts of the law, and permiſſions of the law. They anſwere, that though indeed the law cōmādeth not a man yet it permitteth him to beate his wife. Their reaſon is becauſe it ſetteth down no preciſe penalty in ſuch a caſe: & whatſoever the law doth tollerate is not vnlawful, and therefore this action alſo is lawful, though not by precept of the lawe yet by permiſſion of the law. Whereunto my reply is, firſt, to ſaie that the law ſetteth downe no preciſe puniſhment in this caſe is a propoſitiō not ſimply true, for the reaſons before in my firſt reaſon alleaged. Againe that whatſoever the law doth tollerate is lawful, I hold it to bee a poſition abſolutly falſe. The law herein ſhalbe iudge of the law; which ſaith that thoſe things are not without vice (therefore vnlawfull) which are permitted or pardoned by the law and not commanded. The law omitteth ſome things in ſome good reſpects: And thoſe things which we omit (ſaith S. *Chryſoſtome*,) we vnwillingly permit, & what wee vnwillingly permit, we by no meanes would haue committed, but this only we do becauſe we cannot as we would reſtraine the vnbridled affections of the many. Many things therfore are permitted by the law vpon neceſſitie: many things pardoned by the law vpō indulgēcy, which yet are directly againſt good manners, and ſimply ſins in themſelues. I wil inſtāce the cauſe. A widdow that remarrieth within her yeere of mourning, is by the law free frō in-

famie,

famie. but by the lawe also adiudged vnworthie of matrimonial dignity. A virgin that espouseth her selfe without her parentes consent, is by the lawe lawfully; yet by the law also vnhonestly espoused. A husband taking his wife in adultery might lawefully kill her, yet not without the guilte of hainous offence. Lastly the Jewes might lawfully craue a bill of divorce, and put away their wiues vpon any mislike: But Christ tels them it was granted by *Moses* for the hardnes of their hart; being yet a thing most vnlawful, and therfore not so from the beginning. Jn which, and al other cases of like nature, though an evil custome or a peculiar permission may saue a man from the punishment of the law, yet it can never cleare him from the vnlawful act.

And here I purposely omit many eminent and pregnant proofes which hereafter vpon occasion may be added. For what neede I to light so manie torches to the noone day; or propose such multiplicity of reasons to proue a truth so manifest? Let it suffice that hitherto I haue made plea in mine adversaries faculty, & through the firmnes of the cause confirmed mine assertion. Jt is now time to remoue the tents, and gather my selfe within the confines of mine own professiō. Not fearing to be tried herein by any trial; especially this the highest of al trials; where God is the iudge: his worde the law: his Saints & Angels the witnesses, & eternall verity which never doth deceiue, nor can ever be deceived attends vpon the sentence.

Chapt. 5.

The same evinced by the law of God.

NOw here towards the evening of the day & end of my iorney I must craue leaue to rest my selfe a while and entertaine my reader with historicall discourse: to sit me downe in the bloomy shade of *Paradise*, & contēplate the monuments both of womans first creation, & first institution of her marriage. For in the infancie of al things, when God had framed the worlds cōpasse, and bespangled it with glittering starres: when he had fastened the center of the earth, and girte it about with chrystal flowds, when hee had finished his glorious worke, and [c] deputed mā his last creature, to be the cōmander of his new-made world. At length he took a general surview of his labors, and founde them al the fit remainders of so perfit a workeman. Only man was excepted: who was yet but a-lone creature, [d] without any cōpaniō to whō he might cōmunicate his ioies, or impart his sorrow; or [e] of whom he could either hope for cōfort in his life, or expect continuance of his posterity. [f] So that Man seemed not more happy in his ample dominion, then vnfortunate in his solitarie estate. For what could the [g] subiection of al things profit him? Wherein could the pleasures of paradise delight him? What ioy could hee take in his angelical perfection, when hee had none to conuerse withal, but with beasts and trees, & stones,

[c] Gen. 1. 28.

[d] Ruper. in 1. l. de Trin & eius operibus.

[e] S. Tertul. lib. 2. adver. Marcion.

[f] Vide sequenti pagina.

[g] Iosephus Antiq lib. 1 cap. 2.

or such, who could nether vnderstand his reports, or returne him contented answeres? Wherefore he who before saw al his works were good, sawe now that it was not good for man to be alone: but said [h] *Let vs make him a helper like vnto himselfe.* Where the all-eternal creator, who created all other things in a trice of time, for [i] he but spake the word and they were made, doth [k] take a deliberation as it were, and calleth to councel the heavenly trinity: to [l] shew that he had in hand a more divine worke, and was to frame a creature of higher dignitie. [m] He taketh reason to his assistance and wisdome, to manifest that now he was in travel of a reasonable essence, and such an one who was capable of wisdome. And look in what glorious sort as he before proceeded in the creatiō of man, the same likewise he now followeth in the creation of woman; whom he made as an equal associat and fellow-helper for man. For so indeed [n] God pleased to cal her name who best knew her nature.

[h] S. Basilius hom. 11. in Genesin.
[i] Gen. 2. 18.
[k] Gen. 1.
[l] S. Greg. mor li. 9. c. 27.
[m] S. Basil. hom. 9. in Gen.
[n] Orig. hom. 1. in Gen.

Poore and forlorned Adam, let the world now judge whether thou thē needest not a helper, whē being the sole heire vnto the worlds diadem, thou haddest not so much as a friend to speake vnto, or a seruant to commande.

[p] *No bended knee did do thee homage then,*
Nor creeping courtier fawne vpon thy state:
Beasts were thy savage guarde insteed of men,
VVhose sensles sense could neither loue nor hate.

Yet againe most blessed and fortunate *Adam*: God out of thee created a helper for thee, more dutiful

[o] Gen. 2. 18
[p] Translat. ex Prud. Nullus adorabat flexo tum poplite regem, &c.

then any servant, more deare thē any friend. That [q] whatsoever was yet deficient to the perfectiō of thy felicitie, might in this last addition be fully accomplished. That insteede of solitarinesse thou mightest inioy a ioyful companion, and in lewe of barrennesse thou mightest eternally be honoured for the worlds grandsire. This was thy last, but thy greatest of any mortal indowment. [r] Neither was it without cause that shee was last of al made. For as a princesse preparing to come vnto her imperial citie, hath her herbingers sent before, her house adorned & beautified, her courte replenished, her attendants ready, and al things for her entertainement prepared: So it was convenient that before the Queene of the world was created, the world should first be perfited, [s] Paradice the Metropolitan citie of her residence finished, and al things els ready furnished to her hands.

Thus God vouchsafed to honour the first birth of his fairest creature, nothing at all lesse then that of man: and in some things also farre beyond him. [a] *Adam* was moulded out of the dusty clay of the earth: [b] she was framed out of the purified body of man. [c] Neither was shee made of the lowest part, that so shee might seeme his inferiour: nor out of the highest, that therein she might challendge superioritie: but out of the middle of his bodie, of a ribbe of his side, that thereby shee might appeare his equal, and be taken as his fellow-helper. Of a [d] ribbe also from his left side, where the heart as in his privie chamber resteth it selfe, & which the

arme

[q] Hugo de S.V. in Gen. 4.

[r] S. Chryso. hom. 8. in Gen. Damascen. in 2. l. de Gen. 12.

[s] Ioseph. li. 1. antiq. c. 2. Tertullianus lib. 2. adversus Marcionem.

[a] Gen. 2. 7.

[b] Gen. 2. 22.

[c] P. Lomba. 2. dis. 18.

[d] S. Aug. 12 de Civitat. Dei. ca. 21. & 26.

arme as his beloved darling naturally imbraceth: to teach obdurate mã, that woman is the Goddes to whom he ought to sacrifice the loue of his hart: That shee the Saint on whõ he should bestow the chast imbracemẽts of his armes. Or thus much els to intimate,[e] that as it is woman only whose loue should inherit the hart of mã: so it is especially wo mã whose defence should merit the arme of man.

[e] S. Basil. hom. 12. in Gen.

Woman therefore by the divine power of creation was made of man: and [f] man by a strange kinde of *Metamorphosis* converted into woman. For when that dead sleepe had seized on *Adam*, and God had taken fourth his ribbe,[g] he closed vp the breach with tender flesh insteede of the harde bone: To the end that as his heart had now a more soft pillowe to recline it selfe vpon, so his minde should become more mollified: and insteede of its natural fiercenesse begin to assume a natural mildnesse. Which speedily tooke effect. For assoone as he was awaked, hee acknowledged himselfe devided, & turning vnto this new creature perceived himselfe imparted vnto her. Wherefore his first words and morning-song, were words of amity, & a song of loue. [h] *This now is bone of my bone, & flesh of my flesh.*

[f] Gil. ant. interp. in Gen. 1

[g] Idem ibid. & Brunus in 1. Gen.

[h] Gen. 2. 23.

[i] *For God so liuely grav'd vpon this bone*
All Adams beauties; that but hardly one
Could haue the lover from his loue discride,
Or known the bridegrome from his gentle bride;
Saving that shee had a more smiling eie,
A smoother chinne, a cheeke of deeper die:

[i] Transl. ex Bart. per I. Silvest. in opere die. 6.

A fainter voice: a more enticing face:
A deeper tresse: a more delighting grace:
And in her bosom more then Lily white,
Two swelling mounts of Ivorie panting light.
Source of al ioies sweet heshee-coupled one
Thy sacred birth I never thinke vpon
But (ravisht) I admire how God did then
Make two of one, and one of two againe.

For no sooner were these of one divided into two, and made distinct and personal: but streight waie againe they were of two contracted into one, and made the same and Jndividuall. Their creatiō was presently accompanied with institution of their marriage; wherein *Adā* receiued his owne againe with rich advantage. Hee lost ([a] as far as we read) but a bare bone: [b] He received it againe branched into many bones, bewrapped vp in tender flesh, twisted on curious ioints, ful of liuely spirits, flowing with youthful bloud, characteriz'd with azure veines, in proportiō ablolute, beautiful in colour, louely to be seene, louely to be talk'd withal, like in al things. [c] He lost it without any sense of paine; he receiv'd it againe with an extasie of ioy. Jn regard of which his happy fortunes, he established for himselfe & al succeeding ages an eternall law. [d] *Therefore shall man leaue his father and mother, and cleaue vnto his wife, and they two shall bee one flesh.* This was his Hymineal song, this was the first statute of *Adam* made here in Paradise when hee was yet in the state of innocency: whē he was fresh and pure from his creation: and (as the Angels thē

[a] Gen 2. 21
[b] S. Damascenus in l. 2 ad Gen.
[c] Pererius in hunc locum, & Brunus ibid.
[d] Gen. 2. 24

ſelues)in Chriſtal perfection. [e] Then was not his reaſon ouercaſt with any clowds of ſenſuality:his iudgment not tainted of errour: his cōſcience not ſtained with ſin:the eie of his vnderſtanding clear: the propenſion of his wil free: and therefore then was his law moſt exquiſite,and his words the true oracles of fidelity. In this ſo abſolute and Angelical an eſtate,which now the nature of man can no waies reach vnto, ſee how the protoplaſt and firſt venturer on marriage ratifieth the amiable bond, and indiſſulable knot,the firme coniunction, and perfit vnion of Man and wife. *Man ſhall leaue his father and mother and cleaue vnto his wife.* [f] Parents(there is no man doubts) are to be regarded with al filial and reverential duty: They ſhould be the ſecond Gods in our honour,as they are the ſeconde cauſes of our being. Yet as though there were a *neſcio quid* in marriage,ſome higher myſterie,and a relation more eſſential, wee are authorized to relinquiſh them,(and therfore much more al other friends and acquaintance, or whatſoever loue,the loue of God only excepted) to liue vnto our companion who is our ſecond ſelfe. An abſolute law you ſee for *Adam* and man his poſteritie; without condition with *Eue* and woman her ſucceſſion. It may be,his prophetical ſoule ſawe that the future obduritie of man would proue to bee ſo ſtony,as it might ſtand in need of lawes to mollifie it:But womans nature to be ſo gentle, that her louing affection woulde eaſilie prevent any lawe of loue.

[e] Damaſcen. in lib 2.ad Gen.

[f] Exod.20.

And

[b] S.Chryso. t.1.hom 58 in Genes.

And in this the nearest of all neare affinities if [a] *Concorde* be our protector, though we liue not in the glory of the world; though we bee as poore as imagination can conceiue; though fortune doe in al things the worst she can do: Notwithstanding yet we haue an *Asylū* at home or refuge, whervnto when we retire our selues, wee are sure to finde loue waiting at the gate to welcome vs, and true contentment within to entertaine vs. The coūsel-house may proue distastful vnto vs: The citie may chāce deride vs: the court peradventure not smile vpon vs: the fields through solitarines may breede our melancholy: the streetes through popularity may displease vs: al things abroade may not relish so wel with vs. Yet our comfort may be, at home wee haue soveraigne physicke for every diseale of the minde, a present medicine for every maladie, which is *loue*, and *contentment*.

But where *Discorde* raignes, though thy possessions were limited with the bounds of the worlde; though thy attēdantes as numberles as *Xerxes* armie; & thy house as glorious as *Salomons* temple, yet al this is but beggarly riches, or a rich beggarie, whereas thy minde which is the seat of true peace and content, is inhabited by the outragious spirit of strife & contention. Suppose *fortune* were thy Minion, and gaue thee the whole world at cōmande: let the rich *Indies* guilde thee with gold, & the sweet *Arabia* perfume thee with odours: let the sea, and aire, and land, bring delicates vnto thy table; & let Ivory beds inshrine thee from the dis-

mal

mall night. Yet when thou returnest home vnto thine owne bosome, there shalt thou finde a hel of torments, and that bitter roote of the *Colliquintida* of strife which impoisons al the rest.

Farre from the example of this first institution was any such enormity. It was here decreed [d] *They two shalbe one flesh.* Here was an vnion proclaim'd, their bodies are one flesh, their soules one spirite: themselues no more distinctly two, but perfectly one. And if we may be so bold to draw the comparison with al reverēce to mortal mā frō the immortal God: As their Creator is devided in the trinitie of persōs, yet stil remaineth one only God in essence: so these his creatures were distinguished in the duallity of persons, yet stil should they abide as only *Individuū* in nature. On this bargaine our first parents agreed, and this bargaine they truelie performed. For as then the soule of mā as the garden of paradice was enameled only with the flowers of *vertue*: no thissels were then growing, no thornes were planted: *Passion* the mother was not yet borne, nor *vice* her daughter hitherto begotten. This was the age whereof we haue read

[d] Gen. 2. 24

[e] The first, & best of times were pure: a goldē age:
Next to the Gods: & fardest frō tēpestuous rage
Of vice. No other Empres of the world was known
As yet, but sacred vertue: shee then rul'd alone.
Then was eternall spring: the earth with richest flowers
VVas alwaies richly clad: which (when the christall showers
Perform'd their morning sacrifices) gaue such breath,
As though the Gods had daiely new perfum'd the earth.

[e] Descriptio aurei seculi translata ex Ovid. & alijs per authorem.

The sister aire a virgin for the piercing gunne:
The mother earth not yet was wounded by her sonne
The iron instrument: The rugged Oceans backe
Not sadled with the Pine to beare the Marchant packe.
Yet then the earth, the sea, the aire, vntouch'd did yeeld
More fruit: then labour'd now doth aire, or sea, or field.
Rivers of milke & wine from out each fountaine ran;
The herbes and trees drop'd hony for the foode of man.
Bellona *had not yet in sanguine field displaide*
Her sable armes: nor Vulcan *on his anvill plaide*
Musicke vnto the Gods, whiles forged was the sword
Which now with sharpe revenge seconds each hasty word.
No bended trumpet yet had taught the furious steede
To keepe his circle, and the crackling speare to guide
Against his adverse crest. No warres were then, no strife
But in this golden age, they liv'd a golden life.

And paralel also vnto the purity of this goldē age was the perfection of mans & womans soule. For whē their bodies were first framed as a picture of wrought waxe, or an image of hewen stone, God breathed therevnto a liuely soule, which he stiled the breath of life. And that [b] spirit being of an aëreal substance & (as it were) angelical essence, diffused it selfe into each part, giving motion, sense and reason vnto the whole. Now in this naturall marriage of soule and body, the soule actuated the body, the body supported the soule. The soule brought with her a rich dowry for the body, quick apprehension, deepe vnderstanding, and a treasury frought with memory. The body, a faire possession for the soule: he received her within the strōg

[b] Arist. li. 1. de anima. cap. 6.

wals

wals of his house, seated her in the warlike castel of his heart; fortified her with the thicke bulworke of his breast; attended her with waiting faculties as a family of so many servãts; made his eies her watch men; his tongue her orator; his hands her champions; his feet her lackies; his cõmon parts her common vassals: some for admitting of nourishment, the mouth to receiue it, the teeth to grinde it, the pallate to rellish it, the fornace of the stomacke to concoct it, the fan of the liver to purifie it, the ferry of the vaines to warse it through the whole cõtinẽt of this litle world. Some againe for avoidãce of excrement, the eies as cõducts of the head, the nostrils as the sluices of the braine, the eares as channels of other ordure, & the hidden members as fit organs for such hidden offices.

Now whõsoever it pleaseth with the eie of iudgment to take review of my travels hitherto in this part; Of womans first creation, equal vnto mãs, having the same maker, the same manner of making: better then mans, because formed of a better substãce, in a place more excellẽt, & at a more sacred time. Of the original of marriage; equal to both, in asmuch as both were one flesh, one nature: more expresly binding the man, because the law was expresly confirmed by the man vnto the womã, not expresly reconfirmed by the womã vnto the mã. Lastly of the purity of this age, frõ whẽce all these testimonies are drawn: He wil easily cõclude what I haue labored to cõfirme; That man & wife here lived a peaceable life, they inioied a loving vnion, they lived in pure amity. If ever there were made an absolute law, if ever statute of such perfection, as neither errour coulde corrupte it, nor vice depraue it, this (we are sure) was it, where God at the first creation was the lawgiver, and man in his first perfection the lawe-receiver. Whereas therefore our imitation is to bee drawne from the best patternes, here may wee rest our selues at the mouth of God, and drawe from out the verie fountaine of truth, the true precepts of this mutuall duetie, both of husbandes towardes their wiues, and wiues againe towardes their husbandes. Beeing indeede all Iniunctions of mutual loue, and perfit amitie: No wordes of rigorous predomination, no thoughte of vnkinde

[a] August. li. de cont. c. 4. preheminence. It was only (saith [a] *Saint Augustine*) a mysterie of vnion, a sacrament of loue, a bonde of fidelitie, a paradise of content, it was the truce of peace for terme of this present life, and the way vnto perfection in that better life to come.

But man (you will saie) by occasion of the woman fell from this integritie, and therefore woman was not afterwardes to expecte from man such dueties of amitie. True it is, the *Serpent* by long perswasions induced her to a delightful sinne of eating the forbidden apple, yet shee shewed a maine resistance; To the Serpents cunning de-

[a] Gen 3. 1. maunde, [a] *VVhy hath God forbidden you to eate of the fruite of the garden?* Shee made a short and sharpe answere, implying a plaine falsification in

his

his close assertion. [b] *VVee eate of the fruite of the garden, but of the fruit of the tree in the middest of Paradise God commaunded vs not to eate, least we shoulde die the death.* From hence shee draue him to his naturall trade of open lying. *You shall not die the death.* Adding therwithal a vaine hope of shamefull knowledge. Thus in a faire combate, for a faire time shee stoode out at staues end with him; till through his stratagems at length he got the glory of the day. Gen.3.2.3 [c] Ibid.v.4.

But *Adam* assoone as the apple was proffered vnto him, did never cast anie doubt, never made question, never demurred on the matter, but streight way tasted the sweetnesse thereof, whose bitter rellish remaines in vs vntil this day. I see no reason then, but in this cause Man was more in fault to bee so suddenlie deceived, then woman who was more hardly drawne therevnto. Especially when that general prohibition of eating this forbidden fruite, was not given vnto woman, [e] *Thou* (saith GOD vnto man) *shalt not eate of the tree of knowledge of good and evill.* And how soeuer [f] S. *Gregorie* hath it, *you shall not eate*, as though it were spoken to both man & woman, yet the original reades it in the singular number: And [h] S. *Austen* taketh awaie the doubt, and telleth vs that by tradition the woman receiued this commandement from the man, not by deliverie from God. This I willingly do grant, & thence also conclude, that by reason thereof, the woman might chaunce more easilie to breake this lawe, then the

[e] Gen.2.17

[f] Greg.l.35 Moral.c.16

[h] Aug. li. 8. Gen. ad literam c.17.

the man; since the al-glorious Maiesty of God that commanded should take deeper effect in man, thē the equallity of persō that related could in the woman, the roaring of a Lyon is more trembled at, then the scritching of an Owle; the commands of a King more powerful thē the words of a silly subiect. And whereas al the fault of our first fall is cōmonly laid vnto womans charge. *Evah* was but in parte the occasion thereof; *Adam* was the sole cause thereof. [a] For had hee observed the commande of God, though shee ten thousand times had broken it, wee had not tasted of death. Wee had never for her fault beene punished, for his only we were. The reason is because he was our first roote, *Evah* and we his after branches, the one being once corrupted, through him only the other withered.

[a] Cōmunis hæc sentētia Interpretum & Scholasticorum.

Howsoever yet the case stood betweene *Adā* & *Eue*, I verily perswade my selfe, that the same serpent, who was the perswader of their first fall, was likewise the first sower of dissention betweene man & wife. Doubtlesse it never proceeded from God, who bound them in so strong a bond of loue. It never proceeded from man, who so strongly established his loue. If neither from God nor from man, from whom then I pray you, but frō the Devil, that grand hater of loue, and lover of hatred? Neither is this position a childe of mine own fancie, [b] or the conceite only of some other far better learned. [c] *S. Chrysostome* is the author, Satan (saith he) cūningly insinuated himselfe into the cōpanie

[b] Hoc enim acutissimè observavit generosissima & doct. fœmina I. Odovena in oratione sua apologetica pro fœminis.

[c] S. Chrys. hom. 57. in 29. Gen.

of

of mā & wife, & craftily disioined their harts whō God before had ioined, whereby strife and contētion do now oftentimes reigne with them insteed of loue & contentment. May it please you therefore that are rigorous husbands vnto your wiues, or such as are maintainers of this conceited opinion, to take some notice of the author therof. A worthy patron (beleeue it) for so vnworthy a practise, a famous founder of so impious a sect. Heauen abhorres it, the earth was not so base to invent it: hel must bee sought, and the Devil founde out for the first broaker thereof. I thinke there is no man so shamelesse but woulde bee ashamed to take his practise from a notorious wicked man. How can you thē be contented to be apprentices in the Devils trade? Were there no other reason in the worlde to disswade men from this impietie, but only this, that it hath the Devill for its author, what reasonable man is there but would abhorre it? But now many manifest authorities out of the worde of God, and practise of al the godlyest men since the worlde beganne: Manie firme testimonies of the ancient fathers, & latter Divines, I am faine for this present to omit, because time and haste of other occasions deny me the Presse. So that to them it cannot now giue light, although I had given them as perfecte life as to anye of the rest.

CHAP.

CHAPT. 6.

MY conclusion therefore shall only bee an earnest request vnto such as are married, that as they are boũd by the word of God, and as they haue impledged their faith vnto the church of God, they seeke to honour this honorable estate. Husbands, that they loue their wiues, as Christ loveth his church: his loue vnto his church is the dearest of al deare loues, such shoulde yours be vnto your wiues. Resolue your consciences of what due authority you haue over your wiues. Try the vtmost of your lawful bounds; never step over into the thorny field of tyrãny, to which the world hath proclaimed a shame, & God hath denoũced a curse. Wiues loue your husbands as the church againe loveth Christ. Its loue vnto Christ, is its greatest glory: so should yours vnto your husbãds. Be you subiect vnto them in things lawfully commanded; shew obedience vnto thẽ where it is due: Both husbands & wiues liue togither one in the vnity of soules and consents as you are pronounced one in the vnity of body and flesh. My last wish is, that this my short treatise may proue such as the temple of the goddest *Viri-placa* in Rome, vnto whom (as [a] *Livie* reports) whatsoever man & wife dissentiously living came to sacrifice: They returned home againe in loue & amity. If my perswasions worke such effect, my labor is amply requited: and their sacrifice of a little time in reading not idlely bestowed.

[a] Liv. hist. ab vrb cond. li. vlt.

FINIS.